THRIVING
from A to Z

Other Books By The Author

Shift Into Thrive: Six Strategies for Women to Unlock the Power of Resiliency
Integrated Talent Management Scorecards: Insights from World-Class Organizations on Demonstrating Value
The Leadership Scorecard
Implementing Training Scorecards

THRIVING from A to Z

Best Practices to Increase Resilience, Satisfaction, and Success

LYNN SCHMIDT, PhD

Copyright © 2018 Lynn Schmidt

ALL RIGHTS RESERVED

No part of this book can be translated, used, or reproduced in any form or by any means, in whole or part, electronic or mechanical, including photocopying, recording, taping, or by any information storage or retrieval system without the express written permission from the author, except for use in brief quotations within critical articles and reviews. For permission requests, please address lschmidt912@hotmail.com or Bobo Publishing.

Published 2019
Printed in the United States of America
ISBN (Paperback): 9780578411033
ISBN (E-Book): 9781733549608
Library of Congress Control Number: 2018915056

Cover Design by Megan Katsanevakis - Hue Creative
Interior Design by Renee Settle - Wild Wisdom

Limits of Liability and Disclaimer of Warranty

The author shall not be liable for your use or misuse of this material. The contents are strictly for informational and educational purposes only.

The purpose of this book is to educate and entertain. The author does not guarantee that anyone following these techniques, strategies, suggestions, or activities will be successful. The author has neither liability nor responsibility to anyone with respect to any loss or damage caused, or alleged to be caused, directly or indirectly by the information contained in this book.

This book is not intended to be a substitute for the medical advice of a licensed physician or mental health professional. The reader should consult with a doctor or mental health professional in any matters relating to his/her health or psychological well-being.

Bobo Publishing
1916 S. Springbrook Lane
Boise, ID 83706

Contents

Introduction	1
Aloneness	5
Balance	10
Creativity	15
Discomfort	20
Empathy	25
Flexibility	30
Gratitude	35
Healthiness	40
Introspection	45
Joyfulness	50
Kindness	55
Learning	60
Meditation	65
Nature	70
Optimism	75
Purpose	80
Questioning	85
Relationships	90
Spirituality	95

*T*enacity	100
*U*niqueness	105
*V*ision	110
*W*ell-being	115
e*X*ploration	120
*Y*ou-ness	125
*Z*est	130
Start Thriving	135
Acknowledgments	139
Notes	140
About the Author	144

A sunflower mandala is a spiritual symbol representing enlightenment, transformation, and wholeness through joy, energy, renewal, and longevity. This book is dedicated to everyone seeking wholeness and desiring to thrive. May this book enlighten and transform you. I wish you a journey filled with joy.

What would life be if we had no courage to attempt anything?

- Vincent Van Gogh, Post-Impressionist painter

Introduction

My mission in life is not merely to survive, but to thrive; and to do so with some passion, some compassion, some humor, and some style.
—Maya Angelou, American writer and poet

Sexually abused and mute for several years as a child, Maya Angelou didn't just survive her challenges. She made an intentional decision to implement the practices necessary to thrive. She spent time alone, reflected, read, listened, and observed. She held jobs that took her out of her comfort zone and pursued goals that enabled her to achieve her purpose in life. She explored the world and traveled extensively. She built relationships with diverse groups of people. And she thrived. Maya Angelou wrote at least twelve books, acted in plays, produced television documentaries, and composed movie scores. Among the many awards she received are a Pulitzer nomination, several Grammys, and the Presidential Medal of Freedom.

Thriving is an intentional choice. When you encounter challenges and adversity, big or small, you typically move into a state of decline. Decline is a negative state of mind. You might experience negative self-talk, anxiety, and low self-esteem. How long you stay in decline will usually vary based on your resilience, or your ability to recover quickly from difficulties. At some point, you will move from decline to survive. Survive is who you were and where you were before the challenging event happened. Life is back to how it was, often with the same issues and challenges.

****

To move from surviving to thriving, you must make an intentional choice to do so. It requires implementing resilience practices for you to learn, grow, and transform. Thriving requires getting out of your comfort zone.

****

If you are using resilience practices before encountering adversity, your time in decline will frequently be shorter, and you'll move past surviving into thriving. You can choose to implement resilience practices to thrive at any time; before, during, and after a challenging experience. Resilient people don't wait for adversity to happen. They proactively implement resilience practices before they encounter challenges.

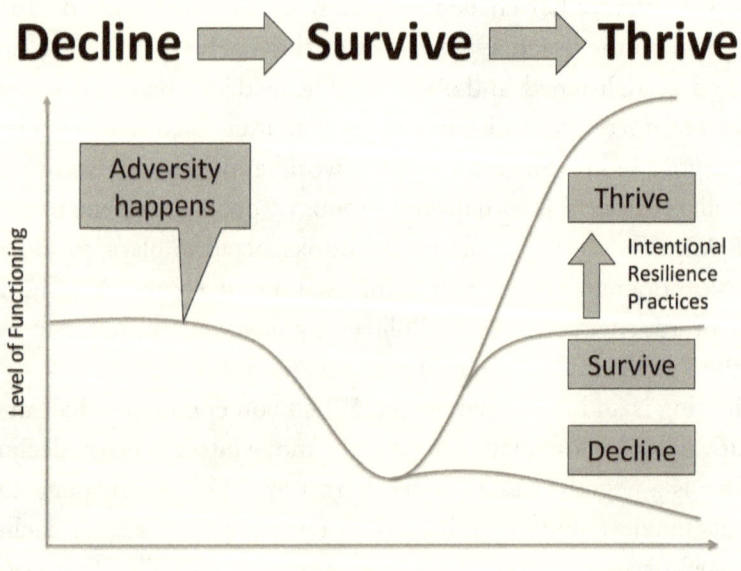

RESILIENCE BEST PRACTICES

Research indicates that there are six resiliency strategies that enable individuals to thrive. Within those six strategies are multiple best practices that build resilience. The six resiliency strategies are:

- Strengthen Support Networks—Proactively increase the breadth and depth of your support networks to help you maintain or regain balance in the midst of adversity.

- Clarify Purpose—Focus on understanding your values, passions, vision, mission, and goals to boost your sense of optimism, align your behavior, and take action.

- Build Self-Awareness—Develop an awareness of your thoughts, emotions, and development needs to improve your capacity to consciously manage your behavior.

- Enhance Self-Care—Improve your physical, emotional, and spiritual well-being to increase your energy and inoculate yourself against stress.

- Actualize Strengths—Maximize your strengths to build confidence, gain the courage to take risks, and achieve greater results.

- Broaden Coping Skills—Strengthen the skills necessary to reframe the challenge and make intentional choices that lead to growth and thriving, not just surviving.

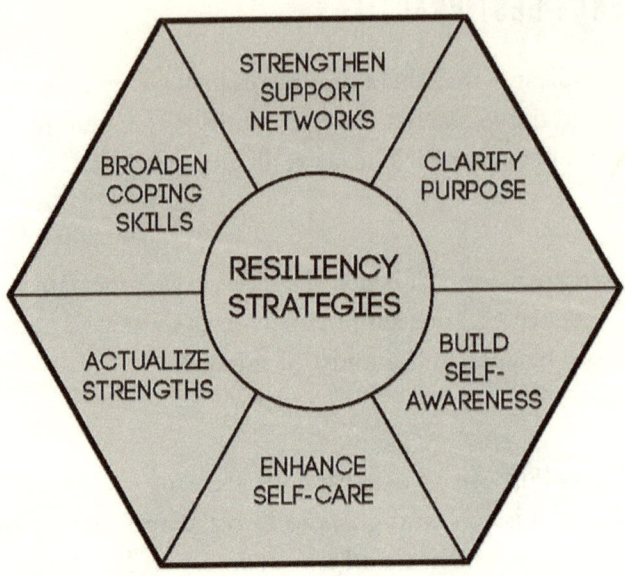

This book delves into the six strategies and provides twenty-six best practices, from A to Z, that are known to increase resilience. You don't need to start working on all twenty-six best practices at the same time. Examine which ones you are currently doing and which ones require your focus. Integrate best practices you want to develop with your strengths. Review the list of best practices and pick two or three that will push you out of your comfort zone. Start with the best practices that will require you to get uncomfortable, learn, and grow.

Each chapter provides an overview of one best practice, tips on how to implement it, reflection activities, and space for journaling. This information will get you started on your journey toward increasing your resilience, satisfaction, and success. The best practices can be used as a guide to coach or mentor others to grow and thrive. As you review the best practices, take notes, design your plan to thrive, and stick with it. You'll be excited about the results you achieve. Make time today to create your most resilient self and thrive.

loneness

Loneliness is a misunderstood aloneness. Aloneness has a beauty and grandeur, a positivity; loneliness is poor, negative, dark, dismal.

—Osho, Indian spiritual leader

Being alone may be one of your greatest fears. We fear it because we don't understand it and misinterpret aloneness for loneliness. Aloneness is a positive practice that you must work on to improve. The better you are at being alone, the more resilient you become. The first aspect of aloneness is relationship based, and the second is activity based. It is important to understand that aloneness does not mean you are solitary or lonely.

****

Aloneness means you enjoy your own company and don't depend on poor relationships or unimportant activities to fill your time.

****

The first aspect of aloneness is our relationships with others. We often fill our time in relationships with people who do not appreciate us or mistreat us simply because we do not want to be alone. This stems from an inability to be comfortable with our own company and entertain ourselves. If you have ever been in a relationship with someone—a friend, partner, spouse, or relative who truly didn't care about you—you know that being with others does not guarantee you won't feel lonely. We stay in these poor relationships because being comfortable yet miserable is less threatening than getting uncomfortable and leaving. As human beings, we want to connect and to live our lives through and with others. We have a relationship, or pack, orientation. Spending time alone means that you will get to know yourself intimately and explore your inner thoughts and feelings. That can be scary.

****

We have to know ourselves to become more resilient. The only way to know yourself is for you to spend quality time with you.

****

The second aspect of aloneness is the unimportant activities we engage in to fill our time and dull our minds. Spending quality time alone does not mean you are by yourself binge-watching a television show or playing video games. Not that there isn't a time and a place for more mindless activities, but that is not how you reap the benefits of being alone.

The recommendation is for you to spend time alone doing physical or mental activities that benefit your health. Regularly spending time alone uninterrupted, not working or using your phone, has multiple benefits for both introverts and extroverts. The benefits include improved moods, intelligence, creativity, and energy. All these benefits lead to increased resilience. Don't let your fear of being lonely, or your resistance to getting to know yourself fully, get in the way of spending quality time alone. While it may be difficult at first, you'll appreciate the benefits.

TIPS FOR PRACTICING ALONENESS

- Explore how much time you spend alone. When practicing aloneness, you are not spending time in the company of others or engaging in activities that don't benefit your physical or mental health.

- Remember that being alone does not equate to being lonely. When you are practicing aloneness, you should feel good about spending time with your best friend, yourself.

- Don't engage in unimportant or mindless activities when practicing aloneness.

- While you may be alone when working, work does not count as an aloneness activity, as it is a required part of your day.

- Spend one hour a day practicing aloneness and engaging in activities to benefit your physical or mental health. Integrate aloneness with other best practices.

- Practicing aloneness may make you feel very uncomfortable at first. Stick with it, as the benefits you experience will make it worth the effort.

ALONENESS REFLECTION ACTIVITIES

- Track the amount of time you spend practicing aloneness for two weeks. Record the date, time, amount of time, and the type of aloneness activities that you do.

- Evaluate your current aloneness practice. You should be spending one hour a day on quality aloneness activities. If not, how can you build that time into your schedule? Are you spending time with others or in activities that aren't beneficial?

- Create a new schedule for practicing aloneness. Consider the days and times. What is the most effective plan for you? What types of activities will benefit you? These should be activities that improve your mood, intelligence, creativity, or energy.

JOURNAL NOTES

Balance

Letting go helps us to live in a more peaceful state of mind and helps restore our balance. It allows others to be responsible for themselves and for us to take our hands off situations that do not belong to us.
—Melody Beattie, author

You have probably been off-balance many times in your life. It happens because we fill our lives with many roles that often have competing priorities. Examples of roles are employee, entrepreneur, father, mother, daughter, son, husband, wife, student, bicyclist, runner, traveler, hiker, author, and musician. For our purposes, the definition of a balanced life is not the ability to focus equally on all the roles in your life all the time. That isn't realistic. The definition of a balanced life is a life where you set boundaries and dedicate the appropriate amount of time to the roles that are important to you. The amount of time spent on your roles can change daily. Your roles can change periodically.

****

Having a balanced life is not about managing your time better; it's about setting boundaries. Setting boundaries takes courage and a willingness to get uncomfortable.

****

You will encounter times when you must push yourself to accomplish tasks for a role. The key is allowing time for recovery by focusing on other roles. That is how you create balance, avoid burnout, build resilience, and thrive. There are two traps you may have to contend with related to your roles. The first trap is the single role trap, where you emphasize one role over the others. One role may feel more comfortable than the others or provide more fulfillment.

When you become consumed by one role, that becomes your persona. For example, you see yourself only as a spouse, parent, job, student, athlete, or artist. You have no, or few, interests outside of that one role. It's unhealthy because you become dependent on that one identity. When things change and that identity goes away, you have nothing left in your life related to that role. Your ability to be resilient is limited, as you have no other interests to create balance in your life.

The second trap is the martyr trap. You may be involved in several roles, but there is at least one that you don't want to do or to do it the way it is defined. You do it anyway, which makes you unhappy and angry. An example is working in a job that requires you to work late and weekends. You do it without complaining, always telling people you can't do anything else because your job keeps you so busy. Your job causes stress, which impacts your physical and mental health. It impedes your ability to thrive. You don't say no or set boundaries that allow you to have balance in your life. When this happens, you become a martyr.

****

Establishing boundaries helps you avoid getting caught in the single role or martyr traps. The roles shouldn't manage you; you should manage the roles.

****

Understanding the roles that are important to you is a first step toward creating balance in your life. You'll need to determine which roles you need to redefine, eliminate, or add, and ensure that you aren't caught in the single role or martyr traps. Creating balance in your life builds resilience, eliminates difficulties caused by the traps, and allows you to overcome life's challenges. While you may never feel that your life is 100 percent balanced, working toward that goal will increase your satisfaction in life.

TIPS FOR PRACTICING BALANCE

- Remember that achieving balance is not about practicing better time management, but about setting boundaries.

- You are living a balanced life when you are spending quality time, not necessarily equal time, in the roles that are most important to you.

- Evaluate your ability to say no and set boundaries.

- Pay attention to the roles you are in when you feel most joyful and explore how to replicate those activities.

- Observe what roles you are in when you feel angry or unhappy and determine how you can better manage those feelings.

- Determine which roles are monopolizing your time. Monitor how much time you spend in various roles.

- Explore if you are in a single role or martyr trap.

BALANCE REFLECTION ACTIVITIES

🌿 List your current roles in order of importance to you. Write a one-paragraph description for each, including the level of satisfaction with the role on a scale of 1 to 10, where 1=low and 10=high. If your satisfaction with a role is low, why is that, and how can you increase role satisfaction? Or does the role need to be reduced or eliminated?

🌿 Explore whether you are in a single role trap. Is there one role that you view as your primary identity? If yes, why? Determine how you can better incorporate the other roles you listed into your life to have balance.

🌿 Identify whether you are in a martyr trap. Does your involvement in any of the roles listed make you unhappy or angry? Do you need to set boundaries by saying no to a role or redefining the responsibilities? If you answered yes, create your plan to set boundaries and establish balance.

🌿 Are there any roles missing that you would like to add to the list? If yes, how will you integrate them?

JOURNAL NOTES

Creativity

Creativity can solve almost any problem. The creative act, the defeat of habit by originality, overcomes everything.
—George Lois, art director and author

You may think that unless you paint like Monet, create films like Spielberg, write music like Mozart, or sing like Beyoncé, you aren't creative. Nothing is further from the truth. We all can be creative. Creativity is described as using your imagination or original concepts to create meaningful new ideas or things. Using creativity within our own lives for artistic endeavors or to problem-solve helps us build resilience and overcome the challenges we encounter.

Creativity is an important practice for increasing resilience. Creativity has been shown to stimulate alpha waves in the brain that correlate with relaxation, and when you are relaxed, you are more likely to have breakthrough ideas. Have you ever wondered why brilliant ideas pop into your head in the shower or while you are taking a walk? It's because you are relaxed and your stress level is low. Other studies show that creative activities raise serotonin levels and decrease anxiety. Engaging in creative activities can lower your stress levels, build resilience, and help you solve problems.

****
> Creativity requires curiosity about the world around you, a willingness to experiment, an acceptance that experimentation may fail, and a desire to try, try again.

****

Unfortunately, the roadblocks to creativity — complacency and fear of failure — get in the way of you moving out of your routine to be creative and solve problems in new ways. It's easy to get caught up in the day-to-day routines. You have your job, family, and friends. At the end of the day, you may be tired and simply want to binge-watch a television show. You become complacent with your life. You take the same route to work, park your car in the same spot, and go to the same grocery store.

****
> As an adult, acceptance of the status quo comes easily, but that acceptance is the killer of creativity. Remember how creative you were as a child, always asking why. You must continue to ask questions as an adult to stimulate your creativity.

****

The other killer of creativity is a fear of failure. As adults, we can become very cautious and concerned about how we appear to our peers. The silliness we are willing to show as children diminishes. Life becomes very serious. Being creative doesn't have to involve taking significant risks, and perfection isn't required. Make time to do activities you enjoyed as a child. Find a hobby. Take a different route to work. Go to a new grocery store. Bake cookies. Play a card game. Get out of your routine to stimulate your brain. These activities will enable you to think about challenges differently and make it easier for you to solve problems. You'll be building resiliency while having fun.

TIPS FOR PRACTICING CREATIVITY

- Remember that being creative doesn't require being an artist. Anyone can be creative.

- Don't let the two killers of creativity, complacency and fear of failure, get in your way.

- Question why you are doing an activity in a certain way and explore how you can improve the process.

- Pick a fun activity you enjoyed as a child and do it today.

- Don't let a desire for perfection hold you back from being creative.

- Examine your routines and change one or two of them. You can start small. Even taking a different route to work or a walk outdoors in a new place will make a difference.

- When you take on a new hobby or project, set aside your fear of failure. Don't let that fear rule you.

- If you have a problem to solve, take a break and do something creative. You'll solve the problem faster.

CREATIVITY REFLECTION ACTIVITIES

🌿 Write down all the activities in your life you believe have become routine. Which ones can you eliminate? Stop doing those routine activities that you can eliminate. This frees up time for more important resilience-building activities.

🌿 Examine your list of routine activities. Which activities can you do differently to create some variety in your life? What is your plan to change how those routine activities get done? Doing things differently will stimulate your brain, as it requires you to think differently.

🌿 Develop a list of creative activities that you enjoyed doing in the past, but haven't done in a long time. Why did you stop doing those activities? Which activities do you want to put back in your life? These activities could be as simple as baking, bicycling, hiking, or photography.

🌿 Brainstorm a list of creative activities that you want to do, but which your routine or fear of failure has kept you from doing. Pick one creative activity from your list and start learning about it. Which creative activity will bring you the most joy? Your next hobby could involve painting, cooking Italian meals, or playing a musical instrument.

JOURNAL NOTES

Discomfort

Hello, fear. Thank you for being here. You're my indication that I'm doing what I need to do.
—Cheryl Strayed, novelist and essayist

You are probably wondering how discomfort can be considered a best practice to build resilience and thrive. You may want to skip this chapter because dealing with discomfort is far too uncomfortable. Both of these responses indicate you are in the right place. It's time for you to take on getting uncomfortable and intentionally bridge the gap between surviving and thriving. Unless, of course, you want to remain where you are. But if that were the case, you wouldn't be reading this book. So, buckle up, and get ready for the ride.

When you experience adversity, your brain moves into decline, a negative place. You might experience a lack of confidence, negative self-talk, anxiety, or unhappiness. Depending on your resilience, you'll move back to survive eventually, where you were before experiencing the challenge. If you remain at survive, the same challenges will recur over time, as nothing has changed, and you'll bounce back and forth between decline and survive.

Moving from surviving to thriving requires that you learn, grow, and transform from the challenging experience. Thriving requires that you intentionally take actions that make you uncomfortable, possibly fearful. Actions that stretch you and move you out of your comfort zone. Experiencing discomfort is how you build the resilience needed to overcome or avoid similar challenges in the future.

****

You don't want to just bounce back from a difficult experience; you want to be a stronger person because of it. Thriving doesn't happen by accident; it's an intentional choice. Thriving takes courage.

****

The problem is that it's easier to be miserable, yet supposedly comfortable, in a predictable life. To survive, but not thrive. Surviving doesn't require getting out of your comfort zone. Surviving doesn't require change. Surviving doesn't require saying hello to your fears. Surviving is getting by. It's why we live in places we don't enjoy, stay in relationships with people who don't respect us, and remain in jobs that make us unhappy. Life is too short to be miserable.

****

Once you face your fears and overcome them, you'll build the resilience needed to do it again. The next time you will be stronger, and it will be less painful to tackle your fears.

****

The ideal approach to thriving is to proactively prepare for the changes you will be implementing in your life that move you from survive to thrive. It's no different than deciding to run a marathon, climb a mountain, or swim the English Channel. Preparation is important to ensure success. You need to decide what changes to make, create a plan, and implement it.

Unfortunately, you don't always have the luxury of being proactive and taking your time. There are times you'll need to say hello to your fears and move forward quickly to cope with adversity. If you focus on proactively building resilience, you'll be strong enough to deal with the surprises that come along. Every best practice in this book has been proven to build resilience, satisfaction, and success. Have some fun getting uncomfortable to build resilience. It will help you successfully tackle life's big challenges.

TIPS FOR PRACTICING DISCOMFORT

- When you decide to get out of your comfort zone, remember that you might feel fear about the change you want to make. Realize you are doing what you need to do to build resilience and create the life you deserve.

- Explore your fears about getting uncomfortable. Ask yourself if your fears are realistic.

- Recognize you aren't alone in exploring your discomfort. Find friends who are working on getting out of their comfort zones and hold each other accountable.

- Keep track of the actions you take to get out of your comfort zone. You'll see how it becomes easier over time.

- Identify when you are in a state of decline. That is an important time to implement resilience-building practices.

- Determine if you are currently in a surviving mode. If so, select one or two actions to move you out of your comfort zone and towards thriving.

- Select other best practices to implement from the list of twenty-six that will take you out of your comfort zone.

DISCOMFORT REFLECTION ACTIVITIES

- Explore what areas of your life are currently in decline. What actions do you need to take to move out of decline to survive? What activities will take you out of your comfort zone and make you fearful? Create a plan and implement resilience best practices to overcome your fears.

- Identify what areas of your life are currently in survive mode. What actions do you need to take to move from surviving to thriving? What actions make you feel uncomfortable or fearful? Implement an action plan to move from surviving to thriving.

- Determine which best practices you should implement proactively. Which of the twenty-six best practices will help you build your resilience and prepare you to overcome challenges? Implement a plan that integrates two or three activities aligned with the best practices you select.

JOURNAL NOTES

Empathy

Learning to stand in somebody else's shoes, to see through their eyes, that's how peace begins. And it's up to you to make that happen. Empathy is a quality of character that can change the world.
—Barack Obama, politician and 44th president of the United States

Demonstrating empathy is a powerful practice that helps you build the strong relationships resilience requires. We often confuse sympathy with empathy. When you feel sympathy, you experience compassion, sorrow, or pity for someone's misfortune. When you are empathetic, you acknowledge your perspective and feelings may be different from another's, and you see beyond your feelings to better understand the other person's perspective and emotions.

****

Empathy is the ability to understand the feelings of others by stepping into their shoes. While you may not fully agree with their feelings, you understand them.

****

Actress Hilary Swank used empathy to prepare for her role as Brandon Teena, a transgendered man who was murdered. She cut off her hair, dressed as a male, and walked the streets of New York for a month to better understand what it's like to be transgendered. Her portrayal helped to increase awareness about the difficulties transgendered people face. Hilary Swank put herself in the shoes of another person. One of the most famous examples of empathy is Gandhi's decision to step into the shoes of the poorest people in India to campaign for Indian independence. He left his life as a lawyer and lived in an ashram for years to understand the experiences of the poor farmers. For most of us, demonstrating empathy will not require that we live the lives of others. It will require that we pause to understand another's life experiences.

You may respond negatively to behavior and feelings you haven't experienced. It's a natural response due to a lack of knowledge and understanding of a new or different situation. Often biases play a role in how you perceive the behavior. Your negative responses can get in the way of establishing healthy relationships and cause you stress as you resist comprehending the differences in perspective. These responses can erode your ability to be resilient and cause unnecessary dissatisfaction in your life. The good news is that empathy is a skill that can be learned.

****

The skills required to be empathetic are listening actively, accepting differing opinions, not judging the other person's perspective, and asking open-ended questions.

****

Demonstrating empathy will broaden your thinking about an issue. By taking the time to understand the other person's behavior and feelings, you'll offload your negative thoughts. There is one cautionary note about empathy for individuals who are highly empathic. It's important to manage your empathetic responses and balance the ability to be objective with your empathy. Don't let your feelings of empathy cloud your ability to make good decisions. Empathy does not mean that you take on everyone's problems. The benefits of practicing empathy are reduced conflict and better relationships leading to increased resilience.

TIPS FOR PRACTICING EMPATHY

- Remember that practicing empathy requires you to be open to understanding the perspective of others.

- Recognize when a different perspective about an issue triggers you. When triggered, you may feel angry or argumentative and want to defend your perspective as right.

- Take time to understand the other person's perspective and broaden your understanding of the issue.

- Put yourself in the other person's shoes by using active listening skills and asking open-ended questions (not those just requiring a yes or no). Active listening requires that you listen to understand, not respond.

- Be open to disagreement and don't be quick to judge the other person's perspective.

- Practicing empathy is hard, yet the benefits outweigh the challenges. As with any skill, it becomes easier over time.

EMPATHY REFLECTION ACTIVITIES

- Write down the differences in perspectives that trigger you. Which differences in opinions, behaviors, beliefs, or feelings make you argumentative and want to defend your perspective as right? Why do these differences trigger you?

- Identify the difference in perspectives that cause you the most difficulties in relationships or create the most negative feelings. Which situations would be improved if you practiced empathy?

- Select your highest priority issue to focus on and create a plan to address it by practicing empathy. What is the situation? What is your perspective? What is the other person's perspective? What skills will you focus on to put yourself in the other person's shoes? What outcomes do you desire?

- Analyze the conversation afterward. What went well? What will you do differently next time? Which skills do you need to improve? Did you achieve your desired outcome? What did you learn about the other person's perspective? How has your perspective changed?

JOURNAL NOTES

Flexibility

If you realize that all things change, there is nothing you will try to hold on to. If you are not afraid of dying, there is nothing you cannot achieve.
—Lao Tzu, philosopher and writer

At the core of our ability to be flexible is our capacity to deal with change. It is natural for individuals to react negatively to change as it can disrupt lives, cause confusion, and increase anxiety. You will be less resilient if you allow change to have a negative impact on your emotions. One thing that is consistent in our lives is change.

****

If you aren't flexible in response to changes, you will constantly be in a state of stress. After each change, you'll decline emotionally and remain there. It will be a struggle to survive, and thriving will be impossible.

****

A key component of Master Resilience Training in the United States Army is mental agility, described as thinking flexibly and accurately, gaining perspective, and being willing to try new strategies. These skills are considered critical for individuals in the military to be resilient under life-threatening situations. Most of us will experience significant changes throughout our lives that require resilience, including job loss, relocation, divorce, the death of a family member, and illness. All of us experience less significant changes daily that require flexibility.

Your response to change can inhibit your ability to be flexible and adapt. While resistance to change is common, if you allow your resistance to be in control, you won't explore different ways to handle the change. You will be stuck in denial and anger about what is happening.

****

Demonstrating flexibility requires you to explore alternative solutions to the change. Flexibility means you select the best alternative for your situation and then move forward in that direction.

****

The key to flexibility is being open to doing things differently than you have in the past. It can mean admitting to mistakes to make improvements. If you are stuck in a comfortable place, you may find it difficult to be open to new ideas. Sometimes you can plan for more significant changes and create various options for how you will handle the change. This will help with adapting to the change emotionally.

Flexibility doesn't mean not having an opinion and going with the flow. Going with the flow or doing what others want to do, but not what is best for you, will only contribute to feelings of dissatisfaction. It's important to provide input if it's a decision you need to make with others and reach an agreement. If you are flexible, you will become more resilient, and it will be easier to adapt to each change. You will bend, but not break.

TIPS FOR PRACTICING FLEXIBILITY

- Remember that your flexibility is affected by your ability to deal with change.

- Realize that change is constant.

- The next time you experience a change, pause and don't respond immediately. Think about a flexible way to respond.

- Remind yourself to be open to new ideas related to changes.

- Stop resisting changes by acknowledging your feelings and the need to move forward.

- Plan for changes whenever possible, and generate a list of options.

- Acknowledge that flexibility does not equate to going with the flow. It's important for you to voice your perspective and come to an agreement on solutions if it's a group decision.

FLEXIBILITY REFLECTION ACTIVITIES

- Think about a recent change you experienced where you weren't as flexible as you could have been. How did you react? Why did you react the way you did? How did you resist the change?

- Explore how you could have responded with more flexibility. What should you have done differently to be more flexible? How would the outcome have changed if you were more flexible?

- List specific actions to take the next time you face change that will allow you to demonstrate flexibility. What will you do and when will you do it? Write down any prompts that will help you remember your plan.

- Do you have a family member or friend you can tell about your plan? If yes, create an accountability partnership with that person. Then you will have someone to help you demonstrate more flexibility.

JOURNAL NOTES

Gratitude

Everything is a gift. The degree to which we are awake to this truth is a measure of our gratefulness, and gratefulness is a measure of our aliveness.
—David Steindl-Rast, Benedictine monk and author

We can practice gratefulness by becoming aware that every moment is a gift, and we can be grateful for the opportunity presented by every moment. That is the key to joyfulness. It doesn't mean we need to be grateful for everything that happens. There are things that we won't be grateful for, such as war, violence, and the death of a loved one. The way we can recognize the opportunities in each moment is to pause and listen, open our eyes to see what is presented, and then do something about the opportunities we are given.

Expressing gratitude has many benefits, including building resilience. Individuals who practice gratefulness on a regular basis feel more joy, sleep better, express more compassion, and have a stronger immune system. These are several attributes needed for resilience. Gratefulness does not mean that you express gratitude only for the momentous events in your life.

>**
>
> A significant characteristic of establishing an ongoing gratitude practice is realizing that there are many moments you currently take for granted that you should be grateful for.
>
> **

If you lose your job or a loved one, you may wonder why you should be grateful. If you examine your life moment by moment, you will find many things for which to express gratitude. You woke up. You have your health. You have hot water for your shower. You have food in the refrigerator. You have a refrigerator. You have friends who care about you. You have a warm coat that fits you perfectly. You have a dog that makes you smile. The list goes on and on. You'll find new things daily that make you grateful.

> **
>
> Recognize both the large and small events in your life as a part of your gratitude practice. That is when you'll realize life is better than you may have thought. That is when you become happier and healthier.
>
> **

A gratitude practice needs to happen on a regular basis. Find a way to express your gratitude daily to experience all the possible benefits. There are many methods to express gratitude, and you'll want to choose the one that works best for you. You can use a gratitude journal and write in it daily. Be sure to pick the time of day that works best for you. Another option is to create a gratitude jar. Write what you are grateful for on slips of paper and place them in the jar each day. You can share what you are grateful for with others by posting your daily thoughts on social media. Whichever method you select, you'll want to review what you have written regularly. That reinforces the positivity of the gratefulness practice.

The benefits of practicing gratefulness are many, and it's a simple habit to develop that requires little time. As with many habits, it can be easy to fall out of the routine. Be sure to pick a method of expressing gratitude that works best for you, and if you become bored with it, move on to another method. Keep your gratitude practice engaging, and you'll stick with it.

TIPS FOR PRACTICING GRATITUDE

- Remember that a gratitude practice is about all the moments in your life. It includes both large and small events, and people as well as things.

- Select a method for expressing gratitude that works best for you. There are many options, including a journal, jar, and sharing on social media.

- Select the best time of day to express gratitude. If you are tired in the evening, maybe the morning would work better.

- Don't overcomplicate the process. Keep it simple and set it up so that it doesn't consume a great deal of your time.

- If you become bored with one method, switch to another. Keep yourself engaged, as that is when you experience the benefits.

- Be specific when you write down the things that make you grateful. Don't say you are grateful for your friends; instead say you are grateful for your friend Sue because she went out of her way to give you a ride to work when your car broke down.

- Periodically review what you have written. Reviewing will reinforce the positive aspects of a gratitude practice and remind you of all the things that make you grateful.

GRATITUDE REFLECTION ACTIVITIES

- Start your gratitude practice by brainstorming. What three or four things are you most grateful for right now? Write down what you are grateful for, and be as specific as possible. Do you have both large and small events, as well as people and things on your list?

- Think about the various methods you can use to express gratefulness. What works best for you? Which method will be easiest for you to make into a daily habit? Pick one method and start using it.

- Explore what time of day works best for you to write down what makes you grateful. Is there one time that will work better than others? Select your time of day.

- Implement your plan and keep it simple. What barriers may get in the way of doing your gratitude practice daily? How can you minimize the impact of the barriers?

- Pay attention to the effect that your gratitude practice has on you. What benefits are you experiencing? You can include these benefits in your gratitude practice.

JOURNAL NOTES

Healthiness

It is health that is real wealth and not pieces of gold and silver.
—Mahatma Gandhi, politician and activist

The practice of healthiness is defined as physical health, including a combination of exercise, diet, and sleep. Other practices that can impact health, including spiritual and emotional well-being, are addressed in other best practices. Your resilience is increased, and stress decreased, by regularly engaging in exercise, eating the right foods, and getting the amount of sleep that you need to function well. Exercise, such as hiking, biking, running, walking, and strength training can increase your energy and reduce physical ailments. A well-balanced diet provides the energy needed to cope with stressful situations and achieve your weight requirements. A good night's sleep works wonders for your mental capacity and ability to think clearly.

****
Each individual's requirements for exercise, diet, and sleep vary. It's up to you to determine the right solutions for you. Your health is the foundation for resilience.
****

If you don't focus on your health, the results can be devastating. When Arianna Huffington was building the Huffington Post, she collapsed due to exhaustion and sleep deprivation. Her collapse was a wake-up call for her to change her lifestyle. She began to get more sleep, moving from four or five hours a night to seven or eight hours. She added exercise into her daily routine, including yoga. Arianna noticed immediate results from making these health-related changes in her life.

While there are no hard-and-fast rules concerning exercise, diet, and sleep, there are general guidelines to follow if you want to thrive, not just survive. As with all such recommendations, it's important to check with your doctor first before making drastic lifestyle changes. Exercising four to five times a week, including both cardio and strength training, is optimal. You should regularly eat a well-balanced diet to include the appropriate mix of carbohydrates, proteins, fats, vitamins, and minerals. The research on sleep says it's important to get seven to eight hours of uninterrupted sleep each night.

****

The best way to create a strong foundation for resilience is to begin with an honest assessment of your healthiness habits related to exercise, diet, and sleep. Then implement a plan to create your most resilient self.

****

Once you have completed your assessment, it's time to decide what changes you need to make to your lifestyle to maintain physical health, decrease stress, and increase energy. Start with small steps down the path toward a healthier life. If you don't exercise at all, then add it in two or three times a week. If you eat a lot of junk food, begin by replacing it with healthy food that is easy to prepare. If you only get four to five hours of sleep a night, turn off the computer and television at least an hour before you go to bed.

Create a progressive plan to increase your focus on exercise, diet, and sleep over a longer period. The practice of healthiness can be hard, especially if you haven't been maintaining your health. Your health, a strong foundation for resilience, is essential to thrive.

TIPS FOR PRACTICING HEALTHINESS

- Remember to start with small changes to your exercise, diet, and sleep habits.

- Consult your doctor before making any significant lifestyle changes.

- Evaluate your current healthiness practices. Conduct a self-assessment of your current habits related to exercise, diet, and sleep.

- Research the areas you want to improve. Read articles and talk to others about their healthiness habits.

- Create and implement a plan to make changes in the areas that are most important to you. Make sure your plan is simple and easy to implement.

- Find a partner who will support you and hold you accountable to your goals. Find someone to exercise with and share diet tips..

- Update your healthiness goals over time to make continued progress.

HEALTHINESS REFLECTION ACTIVITIES

- Write down your initial thoughts concerning your healthiness habits. What aspects of exercise, diet, and sleep are you doing well? Where do you need to improve? What are your strengths? What are your weaknesses?

- Explore what exercise, diet, and sleep strategies have worked for you in the past. Which strategies do you want to replicate and add to your plan? Which strategies didn't work?

- Determine your priorities. Which healthiness habits are currently causing you the most issues due to a lack of focus? Is it most important to focus on exercise, diet, or sleep? Should you focus on a combination of the three?

- Create and implement your action plan. Are your goals easy enough to keep you engaged? Are your goals hard enough to create change? Does your plan progress over time? How will you know the plan is working?

- Identify individuals who can help you with your plan. Is there someone you can ask to exercise with you? Is there someone who can support your diet goals? Is there someone you can tell about your sleep goals?

JOURNAL NOTES

Introspection

The journey into self-love and self-acceptance must begin with self-examination. ... until you take the journey of self-reflection, it is almost impossible to grow or learn in life.
—Iyanla Vanzant, inspirational speaker and author

It's time for you to look deep into your own eyes. To look inward past what everyone sees on the surface and discover what lies beneath. Resilience belongs to individuals who experience difficulties and practice introspection to uncover the truth about what occurred. Resilience requires an analysis of your inner workings so you can thrive in the face of adversity. You need to consider not only what transpired, but your response.

****

Introspection builds resilience when you examine what happened, your role, and lessons learned. The power of introspection is in how you use what you learn about yourself to grow.

****

The practice of introspection is a powerful way to gain control of your life. By taking the time to truly understand what is happening, you can better manage your responses instead of relinquishing control to others. In turn, if there is a lack of focus, introspection can be a waste of time. You'll end up concentrating on surface issues without going deep enough for your reflections to make a difference.

The key to success is to approach a deeper examination of yourself from a place of love and forgiveness. The purpose is not to degrade yourself; no blame or shame is allowed. Introspection will create greater self-awareness and increase your ability to self-manage. Being introspective can help you better understand your strengths and development areas. Then you can determine your actions moving forward. That is how learning and growth occur.

****

Multitasking and short attention spans can make it difficult to be introspective. Introspection requires getting off of your phone and unplugging. It requires that you sit down and reflect.

****

There are many techniques available to help you implement a practice of introspection. Journaling, taking the time to write down your thoughts on a regular basis and then reflect on what you have written, is helpful. Asking what questions has been shown to be more beneficial than why questions when being introspective. Why questions generate a focus on past problems and what questions focus you on discovering new information. Instead of asking "Why did I say that?" ask "What caused me to say that?"

Practicing introspection will positively impact the other best practices. For example, if you are introspective and able to understand what caused you to feel a certain way about an issue, you can increase your ability to put yourself in someone else's shoes and be empathetic. Your next step is to look deep into your eyes and uncover what lies beneath.

TIPS FOR PRACTICING INTROSPECTION

- ❀ Unplug. Put your phone away and disconnect from all forms of outside stimuli, including social media, television, and music. Soak up the silence.

- ❀ Integrate introspection with the aloneness best practice.

- ❀ Reflect on situations that are disrupting your peace.

- ❀ Handwrite your thoughts on paper. You can type your thoughts on your phone or laptop, but don't allow yourself to be distracted by email or phone calls.

- ❀ An alternative is to create an audio recording of your thoughts to listen to or transcribe later.

- ❀ Ask yourself what questions for clarity.

- ❀ Reflect on what you have learned about yourself and others.

- ❀ Talk to another person about what you learned if you have someone in whom you can confide.

INTROSPECTION REFLECTION ACTIVITIES

- Brainstorm two or three situations that are bothering you. Examples are a conflict with another person, a project that didn't work out well, a disagreement with your children, or any type of situation that frustrated you and didn't work out as you had wished. Which situation do you want to reflect on first? What about that situation makes it a priority?

- Pick the right time and place to be introspective about the situation you selected. Make sure you can remain in uninterrupted silence for up to sixty minutes. What is the best way for you to record your thoughts? Writing, typing, or audio recording?

- Jot down a few notes about the situation. What happened? What is the issue? What is bothering you about the situation? Who was involved? What was your response? What could you have done differently? Continue to explore by asking yourself additional questions and noting your responses.

- Conduct several rounds of reflection. Are you going deep enough? Are you exploring your feelings and thoughts? What have you learned? What do you need to do differently in the future?

JOURNAL NOTES

Joyfulness

The joy we feel has little to do with the circumstances of our lives and everything to do with the focus of our lives.
—Russell M. Nelson, religious leader and surgeon

You may think joyfulness and happiness are the same emotion, achieved in the same way, essentially interchangeable. While they are both wonderful feelings, there are distinct differences. The main difference is that one is cultivated internally and the other is caused by external factors. Happiness is externally triggered, tends to be transitory, and is based on your expectations of a person, place, event, or object. Therefore, happiness is fleeting if your expectations aren't met or they change.

****

Joyfulness is developed internally, comes from the heart, and satisfies the soul. You always have access to joy, even in situations that don't make you happy, if you choose to live with that focus.

****

Joyfulness emanates from an understanding of yourself. It springs from feelings of satisfaction, gratitude, and inward peace. Joy is foundational. When you are walking in nature, you'll encounter flowers blooming. Seeing a flower makes you happy. When you get home, you probably won't remember the flower, and the feeling of happiness is gone.

Conversely, your overall experience of walking in nature creates joyfulness. It doesn't matter if flowers are blooming or the sun is shining. Simply being in nature makes you joyful, and that feeling stays with you over time, long after you return from your walk. Because you know that walking in nature brings you joy, you can cultivate it.

****

The party balloon that rises into the sky is happiness. The oxygen that helps the balloon rise in the sky, and affects many other important aspects of life, is joyfulness. The oxygen remains long after the party balloon is gone.

****

Once you understand the difference between happiness and joyfulness, you can begin to cultivate joy. You must choose joy for it to be in your life. It's easy to let the hustle and bustle of life get in the way of experiencing joy and to instead settle for fleeting happiness. Two of the best practices, introspection and gratitude, can help you focus on joyfulness. Introspection helps you better understand yourself and what brings you joy. Expressing gratitude generates an awareness of what you are thankful for, which creates joyfulness.

Joyfulness has many benefits, both physical and mental. We feel joy in our bodies due to the release of dopamine and serotonin, two types of neurotransmitters in the brain. Those neurotransmitters raise your mood. Cultivating joyfulness increases your resilience and satisfaction with life. It provides endurance and strength to face challenges. Joy can lower your heart rate and reduce stress. It's time to reap the benefits of joyfulness.

TIPS FOR PRACTICING JOYFULNESS

- Remember that happiness is fleeting while joyfulness is constant.

- Understand that joyfulness is not dependent on your circumstances but on how you choose to focus your life.

- Distinguish between what makes you happy and what makes you joyful.

- Think of the simple things that bring you joy, as it's often the simple things in life that are easiest to cultivate.

- Practice introspection to learn more about what makes you joyful.

- Practice gratitude and become aware of what you are thankful for to generate joyfulness.

- Choose joyfulness even when you are impacted by circumstances that cause unhappiness.

- Know that if you cultivate joyfulness, it will be there for you during the difficult times. Some days your joy may come from nothing more specific than being alive.

JOYFULNESS REFLECTION ACTIVITIES

- Brainstorm a list of things that bring you joy. Don't analyze during the brainstorming process or limit how many you list. Spend about twenty minutes brainstorming. Evaluate your list. Do the things on your list make you happy or joyful? Are they fleeting or constant? Do they come from the heart or are they externally focused?

- Narrow down your list to the items that bring you joy. What is missing from your list? Are there things that brought you joy in the past that you want to add to the list? Add anything missing that you want to cultivate.

- For each item on your list, write down ways that you can cultivate the joy. What actions can you take to bring more joy into your life?

- How can you focus on joy even when your circumstances make you unhappy?

JOURNAL NOTES

Kindness

Kind words can be short and easy to speak, but their echoes are truly endless.
—Mother Teresa, Catholic nun and saint

So, what's with all the commotion about kindness? There are kindness clubs, kindness committees, kindness projects, kindness revolutions, and kindness communities. The fastest way to go viral on social media is to do a random act of kindness that gets caught on video. There is a National Random Acts of Kindness Day. Paying things forward has been the subject of countless books, movies, and talk shows. The list of how-to books and articles focused on kindness is limitless. You could conclude from all this focus on kindness that as a society we severely lack the kindness gene. Or is the focus on kindness based on a desire to magnify the impact?

****

Kindness has a powerful impact on both the giver and receiver. Practicing kindness is an incredible resiliency builder.

****

Research has shown that regularly volunteering can increase your life span. Demonstrating kindness enables better stress management, lowers blood pressure, reduces depression, and increases feelings of satisfaction with life. Kindness generates more kindness. Helping others can create connections and bring us joy. There is significant brain research showing that acts of kindness create an upward spiral of well-being. The good news is that demonstrating kindness only requires simple actions. The difficulty lies in our busy schedules, high stress levels, and self-absorption. There is no shortage of information on how to be kind and no lack of organizations that focus on promoting kindness.

We encounter many stories of kindness every day that circulate on social media. There are wonderful tales of how people interrupted their busy schedules to help others. The examples of kindness make us feel good and pull at our heartstrings. Every time there is a catastrophic event, stories surface of how people demonstrated kindness by rescuing others, opening their homes to strangers, and making donations.

****

It's not for us to judge if others are kind enough or if enough kindness fills the world. The only acts of kindness you control are your own. The only question for you to answer is, are you kind enough?

****

Many of the acts of kindness we hear about in the news happen during extreme circumstances and require acts of courage combined with kindness. For most of us, all that is required is simple acts of kindness every day. The list of potential acts of kindness is endless. A few ideas: smile, say hello, compliment others, say thank you, bite your tongue, give someone a handwritten thank-you note, tip well, check in with those you care about, be kind to someone you dislike, and pass along a book you enjoyed reading. It's time for some random acts of kindness.

TIPS FOR PRACTICING KINDNESS

- Remember to keep your acts of kindness simple; don't over-complicate things.

- Engage in activities that have meaning for you.

- Reflect on your recent acts of kindness.

- Create a list of the acts of kindness you typically do.

- Research additional ways to demonstrate kindness.

- Consider adding a volunteer activity to your list if you aren't already engaged in volunteerism.

- Build relationships by selecting activities that allow you to engage with others.

- Combine your focus on kindness with the best practice of joyfulness, because demonstrating kindness creates joy.

KINDNESS REFLECTION ACTIVITIES

- Reflect on the last three to four weeks. Write down all the ways you have demonstrated kindness, both large and small. Review the list. Any surprises? Any activities you hadn't originally thought of as acts of kindness? Which activities had the most meaning for you? Which made you the most uncomfortable?

- Create a list of acts of kindness that you want to do in the upcoming three to four weeks. List acts of kindness you have done in the past that had meaning for you. What new items do you want to do? What are a few ideas that will take you out of your comfort zone? Keep the list simple.

- If you aren't regularly involved in a volunteer activity, select one that is important to you. What type of volunteer activities would you like to take on? Which ones are the most meaningful to you? Which ones work best with your schedule? Pick one volunteer activity to engage in.

- Make time to reflect on how your acts of kindness have worked. What worked well? What do you want to do differently? How do you feel about the activities you are doing? How have others felt? Continue to create lists of ideas for the upcoming weeks and review periodically.

JOURNAL NOTES

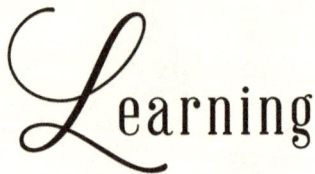earning

You don't learn to walk by following rules. You learn by doing, and by falling over.
—Richard Branson, business magnate and philanthropist

When is the last time someone asked you, "What did you learn today?" When is the last time you asked yourself, "What did I learn today?" Once we leave school, the expectations we have about learning subside. To thrive, you need to acknowledge that you can grow and learn from failure as well as success. Building resilience requires having a growth mindset, leaving your comfort zone to grow, learning from adversity, and applying what you learned to thrive. The foundation of thriving is a belief that learning is a lifelong journey.

****

Treat life like it's your university. Some courses are required, and some are electives. Your classrooms are everywhere. Your teachers are everyone. You create your homework. You decide if you pass or fail.

****

An individual will either have a fixed mindset or a growth mindset. If you have a fixed mindset, you resist growth and believe that your skills and abilities are fixed and unchangeable. If you have a growth mindset, you believe you can adapt and grow, even in the face of adversity. If you believe you can learn and grow from adversity, you probably will. We learn more from failure than success. Our success stems from our strengths and operating in our comfort zones. It's when we step out of our comfort zones that we experience failure and can develop new skills and abilities because of the challenges we experience.

****

> Learning from failure requires courage to acknowledge you aren't perfect. You have to approach failure from a place of love and forgiveness. From there you can open yourself up to the growth opportunities.

****

Another important aspect of lifelong learning is the ability to apply what you learn daily. You'll need to reflect on what you want to learn and what you did learn every day. Focus on how you'll apply what you learned to grow and thrive. You can do this by creating learning goals and reflecting each day on how your goals are progressing. When you establish your learning goals, make sure you are pushing yourself out of your comfort zone. Taking notes or journaling can be very helpful to keep track of progress.

As you create your learning goals, you will want to focus on two areas: goals to maximize your strengths and goals for improvement. We often forget to focus on our strengths and how to maximize what we already do well. This is important, as your strengths are what make you successful. You feel energized when you are using your strengths. Create one or two goals to use your strengths in new ways and one or two goals to improve in areas that require further development. Make sure your goals are specific. Once you have your goals in place, you are ready to start learning.

TIPS FOR PRACTICING LEARNING

- Assess whether you have a fixed mindset or a growth mindset.

- Start simply by asking yourself, "What did I learn today?"

- Identify a few things that you learned recently and how you can integrate those into your life.

- Review your activities and assess if you are doing anything new to take you out of your comfort zone and increase your learning.

- Identify when you failed at something recently, and explore what you learned and applied.

- Practice introspection to help you approach failure with love and forgiveness.

- Practice discomfort and identify development opportunities to engage in that take you out of your comfort zone.

- List two or three strengths to maximize and two or three growth areas for development.

LEARNING REFLECTION ACTIVITIES

- Reflect over the last week or two. What did you learn during this time frame concerning your skills, abilities, or behaviors? What are you doing differently based on what you learned?

- Think back to a recent failure. Why did you fail? What skills, abilities, or behaviors caused the failure? What did you learn from the experience? What are you doing differently because of it? What should you start, stop, or continue based on what you learned? Approach this activity from a place of love and forgiveness.

- Create learning goals that will take you out of your comfort zone. Review what you have learned recently about yourself. What are one or two learning goals that will further maximize your strengths? How will these goals enable you to use your strengths in new and different ways? What are one or two improvement goals for areas that need further development? How will these goals help you apply what you have learned to increase your resilience, satisfaction, and success?

JOURNAL NOTES

Meditation

*Meditation brings wisdom; lack of meditation leaves ignorance.
Know well what leads you forward and what holds you back,
and choose the path that leads to wisdom.*
                                           –Buddha, monk and sage

When you think of meditation, you might envision a person sitting alone cross-legged on the floor in an open space chanting "Ooommm." Wrists are resting on each knee, hands are palm up, and the thumb and forefinger of each hand are slightly touching to form an O. The person's face has a relaxed expression and eyes are closed. This type of meditation is referred to as mantra meditation. Close your eyes and picture someone meditating. Even envisioning someone else meditating can bring forth feelings of peace and serenity.

****

The best investment you can make in yourself is to practice meditation a few minutes a day. No other practice has as great an impact on your quality of life in such a short period.

****

Mantra meditation is one way to meditate and is often the one we see depicted in movies and on television. There are many options to explore when you decide to focus on the practice of meditation. Metta meditation focuses on cultivating an attitude of love and kindness, mindfulness meditation encourages you to remain aware and present in the moment, body scan meditation focuses on progressive relaxation in tense areas of your body, and breath awareness meditation encourages mindful breathing while ignoring other thoughts. Those are only a few of the options available to you. There are also physically active forms of meditation that you can practice, including yoga and walking meditation.

****

Combine the benefits of being in nature with meditation. Unplug and take a walk in nature. Be present in the moment, relax, and let your negative thoughts evaporate.

****

You receive many benefits from practicing meditation that affect your resilience and satisfaction with life. Research on meditation proves that it can calm anxiety, relieve stress, reduce depression, increase self-awareness, generate kindness, enhance attention spans, improve sleep, control pain, and decrease blood pressure. Other studies have shown that meditation may help control addictions and reduce age-related memory loss.

While the benefits of meditation are many, the practice focuses on the moment, not the results. Enjoying the moment is key. The wonderful thing about meditation is that you can do it anywhere and anytime. You don't need special equipment or space. You can begin your practice by dedicating just a few minutes a day, or every other day, to reap the benefits. It's time for you to "Ooommm."

TIPS FOR PRACTICING MEDITATION

- Research the various types of meditation.

- Explore the free and guided meditation apps that are available.

- Try different types of meditation to find the one that best suits you.

- Pick the best time of day for you to devote a few minutes to meditation and decide how frequently you'll meditate. Meditating around the same time of day can make it a habit.

- Decide which location allows you the quiet time you'll need.

- Increase the frequency of your meditation practice until you are practicing once a day.

- Meditate whenever you are feeling stress.

- Don't judge if the meditation session is good or bad; enjoy the moment.

- Accept the thoughts that appear during meditation without anger or judgment.

MEDITATION REFLECTION ACTIVITIES

- Explore implementing a meditation practice. Why do you want to implement a meditation practice? What types of meditation appear to be the best for you to practice? What is the easiest meditation practice for you to start using? What time of day works best for you? What is the optimal location? How frequently do you want to practice initially?

- Try several types of meditation. Which ones allowed you to remain in the moment and why? Which ones were difficult for you to practice? What apps successfully supported your meditation practice? Would a class on meditation help?

- Explore how your meditation practice is working. What aspects of meditation have been helpful and why? What aspects of meditation have been difficult? What changes do you need to make to your meditation practice to implement it successfully?

JOURNAL NOTES

Nature

Those who contemplate the beauty of the earth find reserves of strength that will endure as long as life lasts.
—Rachel Carson, conservationist and author

When is the last time you went forest bathing? Don't interpret the term "forest bathing" too literally. Forest bathing doesn't mean getting naked and taking a bath in the forest, though you could. It means allowing the forest to bathe you with its restorative powers. Forest bathing, or shinrin-yoku, was developed in Japan during the 1980s. The core principle of shinrin-yoku is the belief that taking a relaxed walk in nature will allow you to experience calming, healing, and revitalizing benefits. The type of benefits that will increase your resilience.

Forest bathing's emphasis on the benefits of nature is not a new trend. The advantages of nature have been written about since the beginning of time. Gautama Buddha, Jesus Christ, William Wordsworth, John Muir, Jane Goodall, and many others have shared their experiences with nature.

****

Follow in the footsteps of those who went into nature to find wisdom. Walk into the forest with questions and walk out with answers.

****

Research has shown that leisurely walks in the forest, compared to urban walks, result in a 12 percent decrease in cortisol levels, a 7 percent decrease in sympathetic nerve activity, a 1.4 percent decrease in blood pressure, and a 6 percent decrease in heart rate. The benefits of spending time in nature include reduced stress, improved mood, decreased pain, and a stronger immune system. One study on brain science found that spending four days in nature increased participants' creativity by 50 percent. Some researchers suggest that spending time in nature can reduce mortality.

****

Unplug to reap the greatest benefits nature can provide. Leave the noise behind you and become mindful of all you see, hear, smell, and touch while wandering amongst the trees.

****

An obsession with our jobs, an unwillingness to take vacations, and an attachment to technology are all significant barriers to our ability to enjoy nature. It's easy to become addicted to various forms of technology. Ensuring our jobs and technology aren't a distraction, even for a short walk in a park, can be difficult. To get the real benefits of being in nature, it's necessary to unplug. You don't have to be alone when you are in nature, but you do need to disconnect from distractions.

There are many ways to spend time in nature. You can walk in a city park, sit in a garden, hike a trail, climb a mountain, or wander in a forest. Taking a walk in green space for thirty to forty minutes twice a week is the minimum amount of time you need to receive some of nature's benefits. That's five hours a month. Science has lots of data to support the conclusion that spending time in nature is beneficial for adults and children. However, nature keeps calling you back because of how you feel when you lose yourself in its embrace. Locate those five hours now.

TIPS FOR PRACTICING NATURE

- Assess how much time you currently spend in nature.

- Allow a minimum of thirty or forty minutes, twice a week, to connect with nature. That's only five hours a month.

- Determine the easiest way to spend time in nearby nature on a daily basis. Local parks, neighborhood streets lined with trees, and gardens provide the easiest access.

- Look for nearby locations you can go to for a few hours once a week. Larger parks, rivers, and lakes are great options.

- Identify places that allow you to spend longer times in the wilderness at least once a month. Suggestions are nearby forests, foothills trails, and national parks.

- Explore nature with others and involve friends, family, and pets. Join clubs that focus on outdoor activities.

- Integrate other best practices, including aloneness, creativity, healthiness, introspection, and meditation with your nature practice to receive optimum benefits.

NATURE REFLECTION ACTIVITIES

🌿 Create a list of recent activities that connected you with nature and record the amount of time you spent doing each one. Are you spending a minimum of thirty to forty minutes twice a week in nature? If not, why not? What can you do differently to achieve the minimum weekly recommendation? What nearby nature-based locations can you visit daily?

🌿 Explore how you can increase the amount of time you spend in nature and vary the locations you visit. Where can you go to connect to nature for one to two hours once a week? What do you need to do to incorporate a longer weekly activity into your schedule? How can you involve friends, family, and pets in your explorations of nature?

🌿 Determine what you will do to spend time in the wilderness once a month. Where can you go to connect to the wilderness once a month? What do you need to do to incorporate this time into your schedule? What clubs can you join that will support this goal?

🌿 Select another best practice to integrate with your nature practice. Pick from aloneness, creativity, healthiness, introspection, meditation, or another best practice. How will you integrate the two best practices and what activities will you do? After you implement the combined best practices, reflect on the outcomes and benefits you receive.

JOURNAL NOTES

ptimism

The things you think are the disasters in your life are not the disasters really. Almost anything can be turned around: out of every ditch, a path, if you can only see it.
—Hilary Mantel, novelist and essayist

The question often asked is "Are you an optimist who views the glass as half full, or a pessimist who views the glass as half empty?" Pessimism, or believing the worst will happen, causes a lack of resilience and health problems due to the perpetual negativity. When defining optimism, it's helpful to compare optimism to realism. Optimists have confidence about the future, while realists see situations as they are. Realists often focus on "just the facts."

It's not healthy to be blindly optimistic in all situations. Blind optimism can lead to disappointment. One study places optimism and pessimism at the opposite ends of a continuum with realism in the middle. The study suggests that realistic optimism is the ideal trait. A realistic optimist maintains a positive outlook while considering potential constraints. Other research suggests that optimists are proactive realists. No matter how optimism is defined, the bottom line is that you have to be optimistic to be resilient.

****
Optimists have a positive outlook on life. An optimist finds the silver lining in every situation by acknowledging reality and knowing how to turn a negative situation into a positive one.

****

Research has found that having a positive outlook in difficult situations is the most important predictor of resilience. Vietnam veterans who were prisoners of war and didn't display signs of depression or post-traumatic stress disorder (PTSD) participated in a study. The top characteristic that set them apart from other Vietnam veterans with depression or PTSD was optimism. Another study found that people who focused on understanding their challenges and identifying the positive aspects were healthier over time than those who didn't.

****
If you approach a challenge using a growth mindset, you'll be able to find the silver lining. Building resilience is about using positivity to find ways to learn and grow from adversity.

****

Brain science has found that optimism can increase your life span by almost eight years. Optimism reduces stress and promotes the production of the neurotransmitter dopamine. Dopamine increases happiness and motivation. Optimism can help you reduce depression and overcome the impact of adversity. Practicing optimism doesn't mean you won't have bad days or you shouldn't acknowledge negative feelings. It means you will use your optimism to recover more quickly than someone who isn't optimistic.

The good news is there are techniques that everyone can use to increase their optimism. Like any new habit you are developing, increasing optimism takes time and practice. You will experience failure, and you'll need to be tenacious for optimism to become a habit. Optimism is the number-one predictor of resilience, so there is no time to waste. Begin increasing your optimism today.

TIPS FOR PRACTICING OPTIMISM

- Remember that optimism has been identified as the number-one predictor of resilience.

- Assess if you are an optimist, pessimist, realist, or a combination of two or three traits.

- Identify times you have responded pessimistically to a challenge.

- Think about recent situations where you responded optimistically.

- Determine whether you are an optimist who looks for positive outcomes to address reality or you are often blindly optimistic.

- Identify people whom you believe practice optimism and observe their behavior. Positivity begets positivity.

- Practice optimism by thinking and responding positively while looking for ways you can learn and grow from the challenge. Find the silver lining.

- Eliminate your pessimistic responses by identifying negative thoughts that are biased or exaggerated. Replace those negative thoughts with more positive thoughts.

- Integrate your optimism practice with another best practice such as gratitude, introspection, joyfulness, or meditation.

OPTIMISM REFLECTION ACTIVITIES

- Reflect on two or three recent challenges you experienced. How did you respond? Write down all the responses you had: positive, negative, and realistic. Evaluate how you responded to each challenge. Did you respond effectively? If not, why not? How could you have responded more optimistically?

- Determine what you want to do differently the next time you encounter a challenge. What will you do to acknowledge, yet reduce, your negative thoughts and responses? How will you integrate positivity with realism? What will you do to increase your optimism and respond accordingly? Create a list of actions you'll implement the next time you encounter a challenge and then practice those actions.

- Evaluate how your optimism practice is going. What is working well? Where have you experienced difficulties in being optimistic? What triggers your negativity and how can you eliminate those triggers? Continue improving your optimism practice by updating your list of actions and practicing.

JOURNAL NOTES

Purpose

The soul which has no fixed purpose in life is lost; to be everywhere, is to be nowhere.
—Michel de Montaigne, philosopher and essayist

What is your purpose in life? Many of you will feel overwhelmed by the question. Some of you will have an answer that reflects the past, but not the present. A few of you will be able to answer the question without a moment's hesitation, and it will be your truth. Even if you know what your purpose is, it can be hard to articulate.

****

If you have a purpose in life, you'll be better able to overcome adversity and thrive. You will be more resilient because you are clear on your passions and purposeful on achieving your goals.

****

Don't assume that your purpose in life is your job. They are often two different things, with loose connections that can be hard to define. Even if your profession connects to your purpose, where you work could be irrelevant, as it's what you do that matters. Studies on retirement and mortality have shown that the chances of an early death increase after retirement, indicating there is a risk in only finding meaning in a career. For some people, the end of a career signifies the end of their purpose in life, impacting their health. It's important to revisit the question of purpose when you experience significant changes in your life.

Knowing your purpose in life requires that you understand your values, passions, vision, mission, and goals. Your core values represent the underlying beliefs that motivate your actions and define what matters to you. Examples of core values are achievement, service, family, innovation, and health. Your passions typically come from your core values and describe what you want to do. Examples are working at a nonprofit focused on cancer research, volunteering at a hospice, and writing a book to stimulate innovation. Your vision statement depicts your future desired state. Your mission statement centers on the current year and explains how you will work towards achieving your vision. Your goals are specific and enable you to accomplish your mission.

****

You'll find your purpose at the intersection of your values, passions, and vision. Knowing your purpose provides a road map for the journey called life. As with any journey, there will be roadblocks and detours. Your purpose will keep you on the right path.

****

Having a purpose provides physical, emotional, and psychological benefits. Studies have shown that people who have a strong purpose live longer than those who don't. Centenarians tend to have a strong sense of purpose that acts as a buffer against the risk of mortality. Purpose can have a positive effect on heart disease and prevent Alzheimer's disease. People who focus on their purpose feel more content and fulfilled. One study found that people with a high sense of purpose enjoyed more satisfying relationships. It's time to answer the question "What is your purpose in life?"

TIPS FOR PRACTICING PURPOSE

- Identify your core values.

- Understand the passions and interests that motivate you.

- Review the vision practice and develop a clear sense of vision for your life and career.

- Define your purpose in life by exploring the intersection of your values, passions, and vision.

- Create a brief statement describing your purpose in life.

- Create a mission statement aligned with your values, passions, and vision.

- Implement goals that enable you to accomplish your mission.

- Periodically review your values, passions, vision, and purpose to ensure your life is still in alignment with them. Do this every three to five years, or when you experience significant life changes.

- Update your mission statement and goals annually. You can update your goals more frequently, depending on their time frames.

PURPOSE REFLECTION ACTIVITIES

🌿 Locate a list of core values on the internet or use the core values worksheet in *Shift Into Thrive* to identify your core values. What are three to five peak experiences you've had in the last year? What core values are present in those experiences? Using the list of core values, identify the top five values that reflect what is important to you.

🌿 Identify your passions by listing the various elements in your life, such as volunteer work, exercise, school, travel, and career. You can use the passion wheel found in *Shift Into Thrive* or list up to twelve elements. Which of the elements in your life are you most passionate about? Select five of the twelve that you find most fulfilling.

🌿 Formulate your life vision by reviewing the vision practice. What do you want your life to be like in the future? What are your top five values, and how do you want to see them integrated into your life? What are your top five passions, and what role will they play in your life? Write a vision statement that ties your values, passions, and vision for your life together.

🌿 Describe your life purpose by reviewing the intersection of your values, passions, and vision. What's your reason for getting up in the morning? State your purpose in a brief sentence.

🌿 Create a mission statement and goals for the upcoming year. What do you need to do during the next year to work toward achieving your vision? Your mission statement is a brief paragraph that addresses who, what, when, why, and how. Your goals should be very specific and enable you to accomplish your mission.

JOURNAL NOTES

uestioning

The important thing is not to stop questioning. Curiosity has its own reason for existing.
—Albert Einstein, mathematician and physicist

Have you ever wanted to ask a question but didn't because you were concerned about what others would think? As children, we tend to ask a multitude of questions about everything and anything without worry. It's how we learn and grow. Unfortunately, as we age, we stop asking questions because of a desire not to appear stupid. In school, there are right and wrong answers. Curiosity may not be encouraged and is mistaken for ignorance. As we enter the workforce as adults, it's assumed that being an authority means knowing it all. We are conditioned not to be curious.

****

Without curiosity, we wouldn't have automobiles, the internet, Harry Potter, frescoes on the Sistine Chapel ceiling, or the theory of relativity. Asking questions stimulates innovation, creativity, problem solving, and a deeper understanding of life.

****

At this point, you are probably wondering, "How does being curious and asking questions build resilience?" Well, thank you for the question. Research studies have shown that curiosity builds resilience. As you might expect, asking questions leads to personal growth and academic success by creating a better learning experience, enhancing retention, and increasing motivation. One study reported that curiosity in toddlers leads to a higher intelligence quotient (IQ) in older children.

Studies on aging found that curious older adults live longer and have a decreased likelihood of developing hypertension and diabetes. Intellectual curiosity protects against late-life dementia and can delay the disease by almost a decade. When you are curious, you are willing to take risks and get uncomfortable, instead of trying to control life. Discomfort becomes comfortable, even enjoyable.

****

Curiosity about the people around you will strengthen your relationships and increase your empathy. Asking questions is how you get to know people, and it enables you to put yourself in their shoes.

****

Practicing questioning is fairly straightforward. You ask questions. To become curious and ask questions, be open to new ideas and don't assume anything. Approach question-asking as a fun exercise that will reduce boredom. Get out of your comfort zone and learn new things to increase your curiosity and the need to ask questions. You can integrate questioning with several of the other best practices, including creativity, discomfort, empathy, learning, and relationships. What's the first question you'll ask about something new you want to learn?

TIPS FOR PRACTICING QUESTIONING

- How many questions you ask may depend on the topic and person you are questioning. If it's someone you don't know well, you may want to start with just a few questions.

- When you meet new people, let them know that you enjoy asking questions and that your intent is not to question their capabilities but to learn and grow.

- Get out of your comfort zone and be open to new ideas. New situations will provide you with an opportunity to ask questions.

- Don't make assumptions about anything. Ask questions about everything.

- Don't ever let something bore you; ask questions about it to learn more.

- Don't let your fear of appearing stupid stop you from asking questions. If you have the question, someone else does as well.

- Integrate the questioning practice with other best practices, including creativity, discomfort, empathy, learning, and relationships.

QUESTIONING REFLECTION ACTIVITIES

- Identify a topic that makes you curious. Who is the right person to talk with about the topic? What questions do you want to ask that will enable you to learn more? Write down your questions and meet with the individual. How did the conversation go? How can you continue to learn more about this topic?

- Select an activity that will take you out of your comfort zone. The activity could be a hobby or sport you haven't done before. Who should you talk with to learn more about the activity? Write down your questions about the activity and hold your conversations. What did you learn about the activity? Do you know enough to feel comfortable doing the activity? What are your next steps?

- Identify a person who has a different perspective than you about an issue. What questions should you ask to learn more about the person and the issue? Prepare for the conversation and have your meeting. What did you learn about the person's perspective and the issue? How has your perspective changed based on what you learned? What worked well? What would you do differently next time?

JOURNAL NOTES

elationships

Each friend represents a world in us, a world possibly not born until they arrive, and it is only by this meeting that a new world is born.
—Anaïs Nin, diarist and novelist

Your relationships can build you up or let you down. You develop resilience by proactively strengthening your relationships, both personal and professional. Having strong relationships is what enables you to thrive when you encounter difficult times. While some of the best practices are solely up to you to implement, creating relationships takes two people, and that can make it more difficult.

You want to increase both the depth and breadth of your relationships to thrive. Having relationships with depth refers to the closeness of the relationship. It's important to have a few people you can share your innermost thoughts and feelings with about challenging situations. It's not healthy to keep your feelings to yourself. These individuals provide the emotional support you need during difficult times.

✳✳✳

Reach out to a family member, friend, coach, or therapist when times are tough. Find someone who will listen with empathy and allow you to talk your way out of the darkness.

✳✳✳

Having relationships with breadth refers to the professional networks you establish that support your career goals. The support your professional networks provide include education, collaboration, and mentoring. Your involvement in professional networks should be very intentional. Networking doesn't mean that you join every club and professional organization in your city. Identify two or three critical areas that you are interested in that are important to your purpose. Then select two or three professional organizations to join. Make friends, share best practices, and grow.

****

Professional networks are the stimulus for career growth. Ignoring opportunities to network can be a death sentence for your career. Creating strong networks leads to career success.

****

Malala Yousafzai is the young Pakistani girl who was shot point-blank by Taliban gunmen for trying to improve educational opportunities for girls in her country. She survived to speak to the United Nations about her dreams for girls and was awarded the Nobel Peace Prize. During her difficult recovery, she had the full support of her family. The depth of her relationship with her family enabled her to recover from her injuries and continue her advocacy. She strengthened the breadth of her professional networks by creating a foundation focused on educating girls, participating in speaking engagements, and writing a book about her journey. She has both the depth and breadth she needs in her relationships to thrive.

One of the best ways to ensure you have strong personal and professional relationships is to support others. Giving, in addition to receiving, will have a positive impact on your reputation and deepen the emotional connection you have with others. When you are having a networking meeting with someone ask, "How can I help you?" Proactively build relationships to have the support you need to thrive when difficulties arise.

TIPS FOR PRACTICING RELATIONSHIPS

- Assess the depth of your personal relationships and determine if you have a few people with whom you can share your innermost thoughts and feelings.

- Assess the breadth of your professional relationships and decide if you have the education, collaboration, and mentoring you need to accomplish your goals.

- Determine how to deepen your personal relationships with appropriate individuals.

- List your professional networking interests and goals.

- Identify ways to broaden your professional networks, including two or three professional organizations you want to join.

- Generate ideas for how you can reciprocate and support others.

- Explore the opportunity to grow the breadth of your professional network by having a mentor.

RELATIONSHIPS REFLECTION ACTIVITIES

- Determine how you will get support for a current challenge you are facing. What is a current challenge you want to address? Do you need personal or professional support? What specific help do you need? Who do you already have strong relationships with that can support you?

- Create a plan to acquire the support you need for the challenge identified. Who do you want to talk to? When will you have the discussions? What will you request? What will you offer? What do you hope the outcomes of the meetings are? Hold the meetings and evaluate how they went.

- Identify ways to both deepen and broaden your networks. Brainstorm a list of ideas for both categories. How can you create more depth in your relationships? How can you create more breadth in your networks? Implement actions to proactively create stronger relationships.

JOURNAL NOTES

Spirituality

It isn't until you come to a spiritual understanding of who you are – not necessarily a religious feeling, but deep down, the spirit within – that you can begin to take control.
—Oprah Winfrey, media executive and talk show host

Spirituality is defined differently by each person. People who identify as spiritual tend to explore their inner self, seek personal growth and transformation, believe there is a deeper purpose for their lives, value empathy and kindness, and understand that there is more to the world than material things. Some people tie spirituality to their religious beliefs and participation in organized religious activities. Others gain spirituality by focusing on their inner self through activities such as private prayer, meditation, reflection, and yoga. Still others find spirituality in art, music, and nature. Here the definition of spirituality is intentionally broad to include all those examples.

****

Too much noise can cloud the senses. Spirituality necessitates getting away from the noise to gain a better understanding of your inner life.

****

There is a strong link between spirituality, as defined here, and resilience. Research studies indicate that greater spirituality leads to better physical and mental health. People who practice spirituality recover better after a traumatic experience and cope more effectively with adversity. Both military and Olympic training include spiritual practices to help individuals operate at their highest levels of performance and overcome challenges. Positive correlations have been found between spirituality and several of the other best practices, including joyfulness, optimism, purpose, relationships, and well-being. Spirituality, however it is achieved, is important to your health and well-being.

Many activities help you grow spiritually. Formal religious activities develop spirituality in those affiliated with organized religion. Meditation, mindfulness, yoga, breathing techniques, and self-reflection help you focus on understanding your inner self. Journaling enables you to record the thoughts and feelings you experience when reflecting on spirituality. Reading inspirational stories allows you to understand different spiritual philosophies. Spending time in nature and practicing gratitude helps you live more spiritually.

****

Push pause daily. Stopping to listen to the silence can help you gain perspective on what's important in your spiritual life.

****

The key to spirituality is a willingness to explore your inner self. Spirituality is the repository for your beliefs. The other best practices enable you to embrace and grow your spirituality. Spirituality integrates naturally with the other best practices. Combining a focus on aloneness and introspection with spirituality is a natural blending of best practices that enables you to obtain the benefits of all three. Be creative as you explore how to grow your spirituality. Now it's time to determine which spiritual activities work best for you and how to incorporate them into your life.

TIPS FOR PRACTICING SPIRITUALITY

- Determine how to find thirty to sixty minutes each day to focus on your spiritual practice.

- Integrate spirituality with other best practices for optimum impact.

- Explore your beliefs about your greater purpose in life.

- Evaluate how you demonstrate the belief that there is more to the world than material things.

- Examine your beliefs about personal growth and transformation.

- Reflect on how you want to grow spiritually.

- Decide which two or three best practices you want to integrate with spirituality. Spirituality integrates well with the other best practices, as they provide activities for spiritual growth.

- Regularly rotate the best practices you combine with spirituality. One day you could focus on spirituality combined with gratitude, another day you might combine spirituality with meditation and nature.

SPIRITUALITY REFLECTION ACTIVITIES

- Assess how spiritual you are today. Based on the definition of the spirituality practice, write down your initial thoughts about your spirituality. What activities do you engage in that reflect your spirituality? How do you demonstrate that you are a spiritual person? Ask a close friend or family member to describe your spirituality.

- Explore your beliefs about your deeper purpose. What is your current understanding of your deeper purpose in life? What will you do to gain more knowledge about your deeper purpose? Review the purpose practice and complete the reflection activities.

- Evaluate your beliefs about the idea that there is more to the world than material things. What are your current beliefs about what exists in the world beyond the material? What matters to you that is not material? Write your personal motto about material things and include what matters to you.

- Examine your beliefs about personal growth and transformation. Reflect on your inner self and describe a time when you experienced personal growth and transformation. What changed for you? How does your spirituality tie to the growth you experienced? What are your next steps on the road to growth and transformation, specifically related to spiritual growth?

JOURNAL NOTES

Tenacity

Tenacity is a pretty fair substitute for bravery, and the best form of tenacity I know is expressed in a Danish fur trapper's principle: "The next mile is the only one a person really has to make."
—Eric Sevareid, news journalist and author

Tenacity, persistence, and perseverance have much in common. All three behaviors involve not giving up. It's the approach used and difficulties overcome that differentiate them. If you are persistent, you keep using the same approach even when it doesn't work initially, hoping to achieve success. When you persevere, you keep trying the same approach even if it doesn't work initially, and you overcome a few obstacles along the way to achieve success. When you are tenacious, you try one approach, and if it doesn't work, you try another approach. You keep learning, trying new ideas, and overcoming difficulties until you achieve your goal.

****

The tenacious are internally motivated and committed to their purpose. They push through barriers to overcome challenges, apply what they learn, and achieve their desired results.

****

Let's say you have three cats that want some of your food at dinnertime. Your persistent cat sits on the counter across the room from you and meows continually, stopping only for a second or two when you say "no." Your cat that perseveres sits on the floor next to your chair and meows. You scold this cat and push it away, but it returns, meowing. These two cats might get a bite of your food by persisting and persevering, even though their approach doesn't work initially.

Your *tenacious* cat sits on the counter and meows for a few minutes, not fazed when you say "no." Then this cat moves to the floor next to you and meows, not concerned when you push it away. When you aren't looking, the tenacious cat jumps on the table and grabs a piece of steak, runs behind the couch, and enjoys the rewards of a goal achieved. Tenacity paid off. Lessons were learned, challenges overcome, and results achieved.

****

Tenacity is the ability to focus on a difficult task over a prolonged period while applying different solutions to achieve a higher goal.

****

Resilient people have the tenacity to move forward, not despite the challenges they encounter but because of them. Tenacity builds your resilience, enabling you to recover more quickly after encountering adversity. You don't just survive a difficult situation; you come back stronger. You learn, grow, and thrive. Studies indicate that tenacious people have a strong belief system, focus on what is important, and perceive challenges as an opportunity to learn. Tenacious people respond with optimism when faced with difficulties and don't view failure negatively. Louis Pasteur summed it up aptly, "Let me tell you the secret that has led me to my goal. My strength lies solely in my tenacity."

TIPS FOR PRACTICING TENACITY

- Determine whether you typically practice persistence, perseverance, or tenacity. You may find you don't use any of the behaviors or you use a combination of the three.

- Review the definition of tenacity and explore what behaviors you can increase to become more tenacious.

- Integrate the purpose practice with tenacity to focus your efforts on what matters most to you.

- Identify a long-term goal aligned with your purpose that pushes you out of your comfort zone, and be tenacious in achieving success.

- Integrate the learning practice with tenacity and focus on what you can learn and apply as a result of the challenges you encounter.

- Combine the creativity practice with tenacity to help you generate new solutions to achieve your goals.

- Work with someone who is optimistic and tenacious to achieve a common goal and learn how to increase your optimism and tenacity.

- Reflect on your tenacity practice after implementing a few new behaviors; review what went well and what you want to do differently next time.

TENACITY REFLECTION ACTIVITIES

- Think about a goal you achieved. What did you do to achieve the goal that demonstrated tenacity? What went well and what will you do differently next time? How did you apply principles from the discomfort practice to achieve the goal? How did you use what you learned to create new solutions to achieve your goal?

- Reflect on a goal you did not achieve. How could you have been more tenacious to achieve the goal? What went well and what will you do differently next time? How could the goal have been better aligned with what matters to you most, your purpose?

- Select a goal you are currently working on that aligns with your purpose. What will you do to be more tenacious in achieving this goal? How will you overcome challenges by applying what you learn and creating new solutions to problems? What will you do to get out of your comfort zone? How will you address the fear of failure and be more optimistic? Create an action plan that will enable you to achieve this goal. Periodically reflect on how your plan is going and make changes as necessary.

JOURNAL NOTES

Uniqueness

Always remember that you are absolutely unique. Just like everyone else.
—Margaret Mead, cultural anthropologist

We are all unique, every single one of us. Everyone is diverse, and no two people are the same. The uniqueness practice enables us to thrive when we affirm our uniqueness and the uniqueness of others. You can't be resilient when you don't value your unique qualities and those of others. Affirming our uniqueness is difficult, as from the moment we enter this earth we compare ourselves to others. There is pressure to conform to the standards of the day. We struggle with accepting our individuality and instead try to fit in. Affirming the uniqueness of others is hard because of our implicit and explicit biases. Those biases, or preconceived opinions for or against someone, get in the way of appreciating people for who they are.

****

Welcome and celebrate your uniqueness. Be in control of who and what you are. Use your unique qualities to your benefit and create a life aligned with your purpose.

****

Many qualities make you unique and different from everyone else, in addition to your physical traits and genes. You are one of a kind. Some of the things that set you apart are your culture, experiences, relationships, habits, goals, beliefs, creativity, attitude, intelligence, and personality. Embracing your uniqueness has multiple benefits that aid in increasing resiliency, satisfaction, and success. It's less stressful to be yourself than to try to be someone else. Your creativity will have an opportunity to grow if it's not reined in. You're able to develop stronger relationships when people know the real you. Your self-esteem grows as your true opinions matter. You'll contribute so much more to life if you aren't trying to conform. Dr. Seuss said it best, "Why fit in when you were born to stand out?"

****

It requires courage to affirm your uniqueness and the uniqueness of others. Embrace your individuality and allow others to do the same.

****

You form a first impression of someone in seven seconds. Your first impression is the result of biases that arise from your unique qualities. Your biases are based on the different experiences you've had and shape your worldview. You may be aware of your biases, or they can be implicit, living underground. Unfortunately, it's negative biases that lead to bullying, harassment, and exclusion, which is why people hide their uniqueness. You can't eliminate your biases, but you can become aware of them and manage them. More joy will enter your life when you control your biases and don't allow them to influence your responses.

Your capacity to appreciate uniqueness, yours and others, is foundational to building resilience. It impacts all of your relationships, which are core to thriving. Use empathy and kindness to embrace individuality. Accept who you are and gain control of your life.

TIPS FOR PRACTICING UNIQUENESS

- Understand your uniqueness.

- Know which of your unique qualities you appreciate.

- Determine which of your unique qualities you don't value.

- Explore how you can develop a greater appreciation for your unique characteristics.

- Clarify which of your unique qualities you haven't revealed to others and why.

- Decide how you'll share more of your true self to build better relationships.

- Uncover your explicit and implicit biases, both positive and negative.

- Ascertain how your biases affect your relationships with others.

- Create a plan to manage your biases.

UNIQUENESS REFLECTION ACTIVITIES

- Identify a recent time when you didn't reveal unique qualities to others for the sake of acceptance. What unique qualities did you not want others to know? Why did you need to hide those characteristics? How would you handle a similar situation if it occurred again? What could you do differently to share your uniqueness?

- Explore which of your unique characteristics you haven't used to your benefit. What unique qualities haven't you used fully? Which of those are strengths that would be beneficial in helping you achieve your purpose? What do you need to do differently to use those unique qualities? Create a plan to use those unique characteristics to achieve your goals.

- Uncover your implicit and explicit biases, both positive and negative. Think of a recent situation when you had a negative reaction to someone. What biases do you have that you are aware of and try to manage? As you reflect, what new biases did you discover? What can you do to manage your biases and create better relationships with others?

JOURNAL NOTES

Vision

Have a vision. It is the ability to see the invisible. If you can see the invisible, you can achieve the impossible.
—Shiv Khera, author and speaker

You need a dream to create a vision for your life. Martin Luther King dreamed of racial equality, and he worked to achieve it through his vision of influencing a nation to believe all people are created equal. Mother Teresa dreamed of serving the poor, and she realized it through her vision of comforting the poor, the dying, and the world's most unwanted. Walt Disney dreamed of a place where parents and children could have fun together, and he attained it through his vision of a large, magical amusement park.

The purpose practice provided an overview of how your purpose becomes clearer at the intersection of your values, passions, and vision. The vision practice focuses on a life vision. Having a life vision is so important to resiliency and thriving that vision warrants its own practice. If you take a random approach to life, you will encounter more challenges. To thrive, you need to have a captivating vision of your future.

✳✳✳

> Vision begins with a lofty dream. Your dream is an inspiring picture of the future that invigorates your mind, body, and soul. Your desire to achieve your dream is unstoppable.

✳✳✳

The first step in creating a vision for your life is to find your dream. Your dream shouldn't be about material things that bring short-term satisfaction. Your dream is about living for something greater than yourself. Don't put limits on your dream. What were you put on this earth to achieve? Finding your dream involves exploring how you want to change the world and the legacy you want to leave behind. Identifying your dream requires spending time alone being introspective.

****

A vision provides you with the insight to see past current events to your desired future outcomes. A vision gives you strength to overcome challenges along the way.

****

After you identify your lofty dream, the next step is creating a vision for your life that will enable you to achieve your dream. Life visons are written documents, usually one to two pages, with a focus on the future that creates an inspiring image. A vision includes your aspirations, both personal and professional, and unique qualities. Creating your vision involves accessing your spirituality and exploring your inner self.

The benefits of having a vision for your life are many. A vision focuses your priorities, provides a guide for decision-making, helps you maintain balance, and enables you to think long term. With a vision, you are better able to overcome challenges and be tenacious when times are tough. As George Bernard Shaw so eloquently said, "Life isn't about finding yourself. Life is about creating yourself." It's time to create yourself.

TIPS FOR PRACTICING VISION

- Find your dream. Get introspective and brainstorm dream ideas. Don't put limits on your ideas.

- Review your brainstorm list several times, adding and deleting ideas.

- Select the lofty dream that aligns best with your inner self and purpose.

- Create a vision that provides the direction you need to achieve your dream.

- Remember that a life vision focuses on all aspects of your life, professional and personal.

- Draft your vision. It could be between one and two pages long.

- Share your vision with those that can help you achieve it and provide feedback.

- Make sure your vision focuses on what you want to achieve, not what others want for you.

- Rewrite the final version of your vision. Your vision should take you out of your comfort zone.

The first step in creating a vision for your life is to find your dream. Your dream shouldn't be about material things that bring short-term satisfaction. Your dream is about living for something greater than yourself. Don't put limits on your dream. What were you put on this earth to achieve? Finding your dream involves exploring how you want to change the world and the legacy you want to leave behind. Identifying your dream requires spending time alone being introspective.

****

A vision provides you with the insight to see past current events to your desired future outcomes. A vision gives you strength to overcome challenges along the way.

****

After you identify your lofty dream, the next step is creating a vision for your life that will enable you to achieve your dream. Life visons are written documents, usually one to two pages, with a focus on the future that creates an inspiring image. A vision includes your aspirations, both personal and professional, and unique qualities. Creating your vision involves accessing your spirituality and exploring your inner self.

The benefits of having a vision for your life are many. A vision focuses your priorities, provides a guide for decision-making, helps you maintain balance, and enables you to think long term. With a vision, you are better able to overcome challenges and be tenacious when times are tough. As George Bernard Shaw so eloquently said, "Life isn't about finding yourself. Life is about creating yourself." It's time to create yourself.

TIPS FOR PRACTICING VISION

- Find your dream. Get introspective and brainstorm dream ideas. Don't put limits on your ideas.

- Review your brainstorm list several times, adding and deleting ideas.

- Select the lofty dream that aligns best with your inner self and purpose.

- Create a vision that provides the direction you need to achieve your dream.

- Remember that a life vision focuses on all aspects of your life, professional and personal.

- Draft your vision. It could be between one and two pages long.

- Share your vision with those that can help you achieve it and provide feedback.

- Make sure your vision focuses on what you want to achieve, not what others want for you.

- Rewrite the final version of your vision. Your vision should take you out of your comfort zone.

VISION REFLECTION ACTIVITIES

🌿 Get introspective and find your dream. What are your dreams for your future? What impact do you want to have on the world? What legacy do you want to leave behind? Brainstorm dream ideas and don't limit yourself. Review the list and add or delete ideas. Select one dream.

🌿 Create a vision that will enable you to achieve your dream. Brainstorm ideas on what you want to achieve both personally and professionally. What is your family doing? What have you achieved in your career? What is your role in the community? What do you want people to say about you at your funeral? Draft your vision, share it, revise it, and use it as the road map for your life.

🌿 Ask yourself, "What am I here to accomplish?" Evaluate whether your dream and vision will help you to achieve that. Dreams can change. Review your dream and vision periodically to make sure there is still an alignment with your life's purpose.

JOURNAL NOTES

ell-being

Everything can be taken from a man but one thing: the last of human freedoms – to choose one's attitude in any given set of circumstances, to choose one's own way.
—Viktor Frankl, neurologist
and psychiatrist

The practice of well-being focuses on emotional health, while the healthiness practice addresses physical health. When you have a positive sense of well-being, you can meet the demands of daily life. You are more resilient and recover more effectively from adversity. You put bad days in perspective. You choose your attitude and how you will respond to problems. Achieving well-being comes from an awareness of your emotions and what you need in relation to the difficulties you are facing.

****

Don't get trapped in negative emotional responses to problems. Realize your initial emotional response is often not the most effective. Reframe the problem and make decisions that lead to growing and thriving.

****

Well-being involves broadening your coping skills to handle adversity. Focusing on emotional and problem-based coping strategies provides positive solutions to challenges. The first step when faced with adversity is to recognize and manage your emotional reactions. Don't let your emotions manage you; make a conscious choice about how you will respond. You can talk with a friend to get a different perspective on the issue. You can disengage temporarily from the issue through exercise, meditation, and spiritual activities. By talking with a friend or disengaging temporarily, you'll reduce stress and think more clearly. Do what you need to do to get your emotions in check.

The second step in managing adversity is to apply problem-based coping strategies. These strategies include reframing, problem-solving, and taking action. Reframing allows you to shift your perspective and look at the problem more positively. For example, if you lose your job in a downsizing, you can reframe the loss as an opportunity to explore new career opportunities. Problem-solving can give you insights on how to correct mistakes made in the past. Taking action involves identifying your plan to move forward to handle the challenge. The problem-based coping strategies focus on positively applying what you have learned to move forward.

****

Choose to adapt and learn in the face of adversity. Adopt self-talk that is positive and affirming to grow and thrive.

****

It's important to talk to yourself positively with a growth mindset during tough times. Instead of saying, "How could I be so stupid?" say, "What did I learn from this experience?" Increasing positive emotions and decreasing negative emotions through self-talk is critical to successfully overcoming difficulties. Broadening and strengthening your coping skills will reduce stress, build resilience, and increase your positive sense of well-being. Choose your emotional response to adversity.

TIPS FOR PRACTICING WELL-BEING

- Remember that well-being focuses on positive emotional health.

- Choose your attitude and how you respond to problems.

- Recognize that your first emotional response to an issue may not be the best response.

- Use emotional and problem-solving-based coping strategies to overcome adversity.

- Talk with a friend or disengage for some time to gain clarity on an issue.

- Reframe a challenge to learn and grow from the experience.

- Implement problem-solving to discover solutions, and then take action to resolve the issue.

- Use positive self-talk instead of negative self-talk when dealing with adversity.

WELL-BEING REFLECTION ACTIVITIES

- Reflect on your emotional response to a problem you experienced recently. What did you think, say, and do that was positive? What did you think, say, and do that was negative? What messages did your self-talk communicate to you? What will you do differently to manage your emotions and reframe your self-talk the next time you face a problem?

- Identify ways to gain perspective on problems. What strategies have you used in the past to gain perspective on a problem? Examples include exercise, talking to a friend, eating comfort food, and drinking a glass of wine. Which strategies were the most healthy and effective in helping you gain perspective? Which strategies will you use in the future?

- Increase the frequency of positive emotions when faced with difficulties. What positive emotions were triggered by recent experiences? What negative emotions were triggered by recent challenges? What positive emotions do you want to increase and what negative emotions do you want to decrease? What actions will you take to increase your positivity and decrease your negativity?

JOURNAL NOTES

eXploration

You are only given one life, one chance at fully living it ... take risks, believe in your dreams, explore the world and her people, live out loud!
—Danell Lynn, long-distance motorcycle rider

Exploration is more than taking a vacation or going on a trip; it's about going somewhere unfamiliar to discover new things about yourself and others. Exploring requires a mindset that focuses on learning, growth, and transformation through the experiences you have when you go somewhere unfamiliar. Research studies have shown that exploring a new place, near or far, improves your resilience. Exploration reduces stress, increases joyfulness, develops flexibility, enhances creativity, and improves physical health.

****

Become an explorer. Allow exploration to expand your mind and soul. Never return from your adventure the same person you were when the journey began.

****

Exploration gets you out of your comfort zone, an important aspect of building resilience. The personal growth you experience when you leave your comfort zone to explore leads to greater empathy and tolerance. You transform your perspective by learning about other cultures. When you spend time in unfamiliar towns, cities, or countries, you become more accepting of your discomfort in ambiguous situations. Traveling with others can build relationships. Traveling solo increases your confidence and makes it easier to do things alone when you return. The benefits of exploration can be applied to your daily activities when you are back from your trip.

To gain all the benefits associated with exploration, you must have an open mind and a learning agenda. The purpose of exploration is to learn, grow, and transform from new experiences. Don't go to another country hoping to eat the same food you eat in your country. Don't go to a city a few hours away and eat at the same chain restaurant you visit in your hometown. Learn about the customs of diverse cultures as you explore. Visit museums, explore the outdoors, eat different foods, and talk to the local people. Appreciate the uniqueness of the places you visit.

****

The power of exploration comes from how it changes your perspective about yourself and others. The world is yours when you explore with an open mind and a desire to grow.

****

The wonderful thing about exploration is that you don't have to travel far. You can realize the benefits by exploring your town. It's easy to get into a routine of doing activities near your home. There are museums, parks, restaurants, and events you haven't attended in your city. Get out and explore locally. Branch out to nearby cities and other countries. Develop an explorer mindset and seek out the unfamiliar.

TIPS FOR PRACTICING e**X**PLORATION

- Remember that exploration is about going somewhere unfamiliar to learn new things about yourself and others.

- Adopt an explorer mindset by having an open mind and a learning agenda.

- Get out of your comfort zone and seek out the unfamiliar when exploring.

- Travel with others to build relationships.

- Travel solo to get uncomfortable and build confidence.

- Explore your town by going to different restaurants, parks, museums, and events.

- Integrate the exploration practice with one or two other best practices, such as aloneness, creativity, discomfort, learning, and relationships.

- Explore other countries to learn about the uniqueness of diverse cultures and build your flexibility.

eXPLORATION REFLECTION ACTIVITIES

- Select a few local places to explore. What do you want to explore locally? How will the places you select get you out of your comfort zone? What do you want to learn from exploring these new places? How can you ensure you explore with an open mind? When will you begin these new explorations? How will you incorporate reflection on what you learn?

- Explore a different city nearby or a different country. What city or country will you visit that will take you out of your comfort zone? How will you maximize your visit to learn more about local customs and people? What is your learning agenda? How will you ensure you approach the visit with an open mind? Will you travel with others or go solo? When will you reflect on what you learn?

- Integrate the exploration practice with one or two other practices for optimum benefits. What practices will you select to integrate with exploration? Will those practices be strengths or development opportunities? How and when will you integrate the other practices with exploration? How will you record what you learn by integrating the best practices?

JOURNAL NOTES

ou-ness

What's important is that you stay true to yourself. Because when you enter the real world, the most valuable thing you can bring is all your you-ness. ... the world needs more you. And don't let anyone tell you otherwise.
—Bo Burnham, comedian and musician

You may be wondering, "You-ness—is that a real word?" And the answer is, "yes, it is." You-ness is defined as the essence of the self. It's the state of being one's self; the thing that makes you, you. You-ness is more than your unique individual qualities. You-ness is how your unique qualities have integrated to create you. Uniqueness is the individual parts, while you-ness is the whole human being, including virtues and imperfections. You-ness is important to resilience because if you can't be you in your entirety, who can you be? Oscar Wilde was on target when he said, "Be yourself; everyone else is already taken."

✳✳

Your self-concept is how you think about yourself; self-esteem is how you feel about yourself. You need a positive self-concept about your you-ness to have high self-esteem.

✳✳

Studies have shown that psychological health is not possible unless the essential core of a person, the you-ness, is accepted, respected, and loved by one's self and others. This acceptance, respect, and love generate a positive self-concept and higher self-esteem. Higher self-esteem leads to more confidence, kindness, and optimism. It can reduce stress and increase tenacity. Positive self-esteem about your you-ness builds resilience and enables you to reach your goals. You thrive. Individuals with poor self-esteem feel a lack of control, believe the world is a harsh place, and have a victim mentality. Low self-esteem can lead to anxiety, depression, substance abuse, and other mental health disorders.

****

Your you-ness includes your virtues and imperfections. Love yourself in your entirety, faults and all, as perfection is unobtainable.

****

The ability to improve your self-esteem about your you-ness will be important at various times throughout your life. Even if you proactively work on your self-esteem, it can be affected by external factors and decline. Divorce, job loss, project failure, bad grades in school, and a poor performance review are a few of the life events that can cause your self-esteem to drop. You'll want to be on the alert for life events that lead to lower self-esteem and take action to raise it again.

There are many actions you can take to raise your self-esteem. Integrating the you-ness practice with one or two other best practices such as gratitude, healthiness, kindness, meditation, nature, optimism, and well-being is beneficial. Talking with a professional whose job it is to help others with self-esteem issues, such as a therapist, can help. Controlling your inner critic and practicing self-appreciation is a self-esteem booster. Losing your need for perfection and believing in "good enough" is helpful. Understanding that failure is a learning and growth opportunity is critical. In both the good and bad times remember that you deserve to accept, respect, and love your you-ness.

TIPS FOR PRACTICING YOU-NESS

- Remember that you-ness refers to the whole human being, including virtues and imperfections.

- Stay positive by listing your strengths and accomplishments.

- Get control of your inner critic by reframing and making negative statements positive.

- Focus on the healthiness practice and exercise, eat well, and get plenty of sleep.

- Bring more joy into your life by incorporating more fun activities into your day.

- Replace stress with hobbies that require creativity.

- Make time for self-appreciation every day by saying or writing down two things you appreciate about yourself.

- Integrate the you-ness practice with one or two other best practices, including gratitude, healthiness, kindness, meditation, nature, optimism, and well-being.

YOU-NESS REFLECTION ACTIVITIES

🌿 Identify a time when your self-esteem was low. What caused your self-esteem to be low? What were you thinking and feeling at the time? What activities did you do to raise your self-esteem? What went well and what would you do differently next time?

🌿 Reflect on a recent time when your self-esteem was high. What caused your self-esteem to be high? How did you feel about yourself? What actions did you take that created higher self-esteem? What did you learn from this experience that you want to replicate now and in the future?

🌿 Select a current challenge that is having a negative impact on your self-esteem. What can you do to reframe the negativity? What will you do to increase your positive feelings? How can you control your inner critic? Who can support you during this challenging time? When will you take specific actions to raise your self-esteem?

JOURNAL NOTES

Zest

Cultivate the habit of zest. Purposefully seek out the beauty in the seemingly trivial. ... The colors and shapes of the food you eat. The shadows a vase makes on your table. The interesting faces of the people on the bus with you.
—Karen Salmansohn, author and columnist

The outer peel of a lemon or orange that chefs grate into recipes to add gusto is called zest. People who live their lives with gusto or enthusiasm are said to have a zest for life. The zest practice focuses on living life with gusto. In positive psychology, zest is one of the twenty-four human strengths. It's defined as living life with a sense of excitement, anticipation, and energy. When you live life with zest, you approach life as an adventure, and zest gives you the motivation needed to overcome challenges. That is how zest helps you build resilience and thrive. As Benjamin Franklin reportedly quipped, "Some people die at twenty-five and aren't buried until they are seventy-five."

****

Recapture the zest for life you had as a child by approaching each day with wonder. Be in awe of the world around you and find adventures in your backyard.

****

Living life with zest doesn't require getting on a plane or taking long trips to exotic locations. Mini adventures await you right outside your front door. Mini adventures can be found in the ordinary if your eyes are open. Go outside at sunrise and see the beautiful colors in the sky. Feel the texture of the leaves on the trees. Smell the luscious scent of the flowers in the air. Laugh as a squirrel peeks at you from a tree branch. Pause to listen to the sweet chirping of the birds as they say "good morning." You can have mini adventures every day.

****

Develop a zest for life by seeing the extraordinary in the ordinary. Focus on the sensitivity of your five senses to see, hear, smell, touch, and taste with added gusto.

****

Zest contributes to having a healthier and more active life in old age. One study found that older people who report greater enjoyment of life lived five to eight years longer than those who reported less enjoyment of life. Other studies show that zest is related to a higher level of satisfaction with life and a stronger sense of well-being. Having zest has been associated with being passionate about work, resulting in increased work satisfaction. All these benefits add up to increased resilience, satisfaction, and success.

There are several ways to create new habits that increase your zest for life. Engaging in low-impact exercises, meditation, and yoga can improve zest. Increasing the breadth and depth of your relationships contributes to feeling more zestful. Getting out of your daily routine, embarking on adventures, spending time in nature, and adding fun activities to your day promotes zest. Integrating the zest practice with optimism and joyfulness practices will increase your opportunities to be zestful. Have the intent to live your life with zest and show your enthusiasm to the world each day. Zest and joyfulness will be your reward.

TIPS FOR PRACTICING ZEST

- Remember that zest is living your life with more enthusiasm.

- Approach life as an adventure, and zest will motivate you to overcome challenges.

- Find zest by seeing the extraordinary in the ordinary every day.

- Take mini adventures to add zest to your life.

- Integrate zest with joyfulness, healthiness, meditation, or optimism to get optimum results.

- Practice yoga to achieve more zest for life.

- Spend time with positive people whose company you enjoy.

- Add fun activities to your day to increase variety.

- Do an activity in nature that feels like an adventure.

ZEST REFLECTION ACTIVITIES

🌿 Think of situations when you felt enthusiastic about something you were doing. What were the activities? What were your feelings about these activities? Why were you feeling enthusiastic? How can you incorporate these feelings of enthusiasm into your daily life?

🌿 Discover ways to find the extraordinary in the ordinary. What activities can you do that will help you pay more attention to the ordinary things in life? How can you focus on your five senses to see the beauty in everyday items? Select a day to start seeing the extraordinary in the ordinary and pause to observe as you go through the day. Make notes on what you see and feel.

🌿 Plan an activity that you know makes you feel enthusiastic. What is the activity? How do you feel when you do the activity? What creates your enthusiasm? When will you do the activity? Once you do the activity, reflect on how you felt. How can you replicate those feelings daily?

JOURNAL NOTES

Start Thriving

Start by doing what's necessary; then do what's possible; and suddenly you are doing the impossible.
—Francis of Assisi, Catholic friar
and preacher

Thriving from A to Z provides you with information about twenty-six best practices so you can thrive by increasing your resilience, satisfaction, and success. By learning about each best practice, you can decide if it's a practice you want to implement. The tips and reflection activities assist you in working on your action plans, and the journal pages allow you to take notes on your next steps.

You don't need to work on all twenty-six best practices at the same time. Explore which ones are strengths and which ones require your focus. Review the list of best practices and pick two or three that will push you out of your comfort zone. Start with the practices that require you to get uncomfortable, learn, and grow. You may want to integrate practices that are strengths with those you want to develop. Integrating two or three best practices allows you to achieve optimum results. Another approach is to focus on a different best practice each day to experience growth in all practices. One day you focus on being kinder, the next day you practice introspection, and so on.

Use the following Best Practices Checklist to indicate which practices you are going to focus on and integrate. Write down a few action steps to move forward. Then get started and get thriving. Refer to the checklist daily and record your implementation reflections in the journal pages. Update your action steps as you make progress and move from what's necessary to what's possible, and then to the impossible. The impossible will become possible. You'll be thrilled by the differences you'll see in your resilience and satisfaction. Make the time today to create your most successful self, and enjoy the journey. As Mark Twain so fittingly said, "The secret of getting ahead is getting started."

BEST PRACTICES CHECKLIST

- [ ] Aloneness
- [ ] Balance
- [ ] Creativity
- [ ] Discomfort
- [ ] Empathy
- [ ] Flexibility
- [ ] Gratitude
- [ ] Healthiness
- [ ] Introspection
- [ ] Joyfulness
- [ ] Kindness
- [ ] Learning
- [ ] Meditation
- [ ] Nature
- [ ] Optimism
- [ ] Purpose
- [ ] Questioning
- [ ] Relationships
- [ ] Spirituality
- [ ] Tenacity
- [ ] Uniqueness
- [ ] Vision
- [ ] Well-being
- [ ] eXploration
- [ ] You-ness
- [ ] Zest

JOURNAL NOTES

Acknowledgments

Writing a book requires the support and expertise of many people working together for several months to create the final product. I greatly appreciate the contributions of everyone involved in the creation of *Thriving from A to Z*. I received guidance and support from friends, family, and professional acquaintances. Thank you to everyone involved.

I want to extend my appreciation to the men and women who have shared their stories of resilience and thriving with me. Your stories help me gain important insights into what it takes to move from surviving to thriving. I wish all of you the best as you continue on your journeys. I look forward to continuing these discussions as I work to help men and women build resilience and thrive.

I greatly value the contributions provided by all of my friends on social media. Thank you for providing input on your most important resiliency practices, along with suggestions on the book title and cover. A special thank you to my book editor Frank Steele, interior designer Renee Settle, and exterior designer Megan Katsanevakis. Your amazing talents enabled the final product to be a beautiful and engaging book for the world to read. I learned so much from working with all of you. I'm looking forward to our next project together.

To my readers, a heartfelt thank you. Thank you for your interest in building your resilience and creating a life of satisfaction and success. I wish you a journey full of joy as you implement best practices to thrive, not just survive.

Notes

Introduction
Maya Angelou's Story: https://en.m.wikipedia.org/wiki/Maya_Angelou

Thriving and Resilience Strategies: Lynn Schmidt, PhD and Kevin Nourse, PhD, *Shift Into Thrive: Six Strategies for Women to Unlock the Power of Resiliency*, 2016

Aloneness
Loneliness versus Aloneness: https://goodmenproject.com/good-for-the-soul-2/aloneness-is-all-about-wholeness-grmx/

Balance
Martyr: http://www.oprah.com/inspiration/how-to-stop-being-a-martyr

Creativity
Creativity and Resilience: https://www.google.com/amp/s/amp.edutopia.org/article/boosting-resilience-through-creativity

Discomfort
Decline, Survive, and Thrive: Lynn Schmidt, PhD and Kevin Nourse, PhD, *Shift Into Thrive: Six Strategies for Women to Unlock the Power of Resiliency*, 2016

Empathy
Hilary Swank and Gandhi: https://www.romankrznaric.com/outrospection/2010/03/27/407

Flexibility
Master Resilience Training: https://www.sas.upenn.edu/psych/seligman/mrtinarmyjan2011.pdf

Gratitude
Everything is a Gift: https://www.ted.com/talks/david_steindl_rast_want_to_be_happy_be_grateful/up-next?language=en

Benefits of Gratitude: https://www.happify.com/hd/the-science-behind-gratitude/

Healthiness
Exercise, Diet, and Sleep: Lynn Schmidt, PhD and Kevin Nourse, PhD, *Shift Into Thrive: Six Strategies for Women to Unlock the Power of Resiliency*, 2016

Introspection
Asking What: https://www.google.com/amp/s/ideas.ted.com/the-right-way-to-be-introspective-yes-theres-a-wrong-way/amp/

Joyfulness
Joy versus Happiness: https://www.psychologytoday.com/us/blog/pathological-relationships/201212/joy-vs-happiness%3famp

Benefits of Joy: https://www.healthline.com/health/affects-of-joy#1

Kindness
Benefits of Kindness: http://mentalfloss.com/article/71964/7-scientific-benefits-helping-others

Brain Research on Kindness: https://www.psychologytoday.com/us/blog/the-athletes-way/201602/3-specific-ways-helping-others-benefits-your-brain%3famp

Learning
Growth Mindset: Lynn Schmidt, PhD and Kevin Nourse, PhD, *Shift Into Thrive: Six Strategies for Women to Unlock the Power of Resiliency*, 2016

Meditation
Types of Meditation: https://liveanddare.com/types-of-meditation

Benefits of Meditation: https://www.healthline.com/nutrition/12-benefits-of-meditation#section6

Nature
Shinrin-yoku: http://www.shinrin-yoku.org/shinrin-yoku.html

Benefits of Nature: Florence Williams, *The Nature Fix: Why Nature Makes Us Happier, Healthier, and More Creative*, 2018

Optimism
Realism versus Optimism: https://psychcentral.com/lib/realism-and-optimism-do-you-need-both/

Vietnam Veterans Research Study: https://www.google.com/amp/s/www.theatlantic.com/amp/article/273306/

Purpose
Values, Passions, and Vision: Lynn Schmidt, PhD and Kevin Nourse, PhD, *Shift Into Thrive: Six Strategies for Women to Unlock the Power of Resiliency*, 2016

Questioning
Benefits of Questioning: https://medium.com/curiosities/day-2-curious-about-curiosity-5-reasons-a-curious-mind-is-good-for-you-7baff0877569

Relationships
Depth and Breadth of Relationships: Lynn Schmidt, PhD and Kevin Nourse, PhD, *Shift Into Thrive: Six Strategies for Women to Unlock the Power of Resiliency*, 2016

Spirituality
Benefits of Spirituality: https://www.google.com/amp/s/theconversation.com/amp/what-does-it-mean-to-be-spiritual-87236

Tenacity
Tenacity versus Persistence: https://www.emotionallyresilientliving.com/tenacity-growing-beyond-what-you-ever-thought-possible

Benefits of Tenacity: https://chopra.com/articles/resilience-and-grit-how-to-develop-a-growth-mindset

Uniqueness
Unique Traits: https://www.google.com/amp/s/listontap.com/10-things-make-unique/amp/

First Impressions: https://www.psychologicalscience.org/observer/how-many-seconds-to-a-first-impression

Vision
The Big Dreamers: https://www.beliefnet.com/inspiration/galleries/dreams-that-changed-the-world.aspx?p=7

Life Vision: https://corbettbarr.com/how-to-create-a-vision-for-your-life/

Well-being
Emotional and Problem-Based Strategies: Lynn Schmidt, PhD and Kevin Nourse, PhD, *Shift Into Thrive: Six Strategies for Women to Unlock the Power of Resiliency*, 2016

eXploration
Benefits of Exploration: https://www.forbes.com/sites/nomanazish/2018/01/22/five-reasons-why-travel-is-good-for-your-mental-health/amp/

You-ness
Self-esteem: https://www.psychologytoday.com/us/blog/hide-and-seek/201205/building-confidence-and-self-esteem%3famp

Zest
Benefits of Zest: https://www.medicinenet.com/script/main/art.asp?articlekey=176276#

Cultivate Zest: https://advice.shinetext.com/articles/four-ways-to-cultivate-more-zest-in-life/

About the Author

Cam On Photography

Lynn Schmidt, PhD, is a global talent management and organization development consultant with a passion for helping men and women navigate and avoid career setbacks. She is a certified executive coach specializing in assisting men and women create careers accompanied by growth and success. Her career focuses on developing leaders in Fortune 500 companies, non-profits, and academia. Lynn was named one of the Women of the Year by the *Idaho Business Review* for her work with women and resilience.

Lynn is an award-wining author of five books. Her fourth book, *Shift Into Thrive: Six Strategies for Women to Unlock the Power of Resiliency*, won six literary awards and is listed in Inc.com as one of the top 60 books about leadership and business written by women. She is a frequent keynote speaker and presenter at conferences worldwide. She presents on a variety of topics, such as resiliency and thriving, women and career derailment, integrated talent management, leadership development, succession management, and writing nonfiction books.

ABOUT THE AUTHOR

Traveling the world is one of Lynn's passions. She also enjoys long walks in nature, photographing the outdoors, hiking foothills trails, going to new restaurants with friends, and spending time with her two shelties.

Get social with Lynn on social media. You can connect with her at Facebook (www.facebook.com/LynnSchmidtAuthor), LinkedIn (https://www.linkedin.com/in/lynnschmidt), Twitter (@LM_Schmidt), and Instagram (@lynnmschmidt). You can learn more at her website schmidtleadership.com and contact her at lschmidt912@hotmail.com.

A Request

Imagine a world without books. Authors need your support to continue to provide the world with the books we all appreciate. If you enjoyed this book; found it insightful or helpful, then I'd appreciate it if you would post a short review on Amazon. If you belong to Goodreads, you can also post a review there.

Other ways to support authors is to share their posts on social media, tell your family and friends about the book, refer the book to acquaintances, suggest your book club read the book, and ask your library and local bookstore to order the book.

Thank you for your support!

Lynn Schmidt

www.ingramcontent.com/pod-product-compliance
Lightning Source LLC
Chambersburg PA
CBHW021953290426
44108CB00012B/1050